Seismic Stratigraphic Interpretation and Petroleum Exploration

Continuing Education Course Note Series #16

L. F. Brown, Jr.
W. L. Fisher
Bureau of Economic Geology
University of Texas at Austin

The AAPG Continuing Education Course Note Series
is an author-prepared publication of the
AAPG Department of Education.

First Printing, October 1980
Second Printing, November 1982
Third Printing, March 1984
Fourth Printing, July 1985

ISBN: 0-89181-165-6

PREFACE

Interest in the stratigraphic interpretation of seismic reflection data continues to grow. This interest is obvious from industry response during the last few years to continuing education programs on seismic stratigraphy in petroleum exploration. Similarly, this interest has been paralleled by the unprecedented sales of AAPG Memoir 26, "Seismic Stratigraphy--Applications to Hydrocarbon Exploration." Our personal observations indicate that more and more geologists and geophysicists are prospecting worldwide using seismic stratigraphic concepts and methods. Unfortunately, only limited nonproprietary data have been released by the many companies that are involved in its application in exploration.

We assembled this set of continuing education course notes to summarize the current status of this exciting area of basin analysis and prospect evaluation. Our perspective of seismic stratigraphy is based on two decades of involvement in basin analysis and almost a decade of seismic interpretation of depositional systems and component facies. Our work and formulation of our concepts of seismic stratigraphy began in Brazil in the early 1970's with a long-term association with Petroleo Brasileiro (PETROBRAS). We acknowledge the continued support of Petrobras officers and the joint development of concepts and applications with our Brazilian colleagues.

In preparation of the notes, we relied significantly upon reports by P. R. Vail, R. M. Mitchum, Jr., J. B. Sangree, R. G. Todd, J. M. Widmier, J. N. Bubb, W. G. Hatelid and S. Thompson III (Exxon, U.S.A.) published in 1977 in AAPG Memoir 26. These authors made a fundamental contribution to seismic stratigraphy. We gratefully acknowledge their contribution to these notes. More importantly, we acknowledge the impact that their published reports have had worldwide on seismic exploration.

These course notes consist of two parts: (1) "Seismic-Stratigraphic Interpretation of Depositional Systems and Its Role in Petroleum Exploration" and (2) "Geology and Geometry of Depositional Systems." The first set of notes is a relatively comprehensive review of basic concepts and techniques, meshing our concepts with the published contributions by the Exxon explorationists. The notes differ in some respects from chapters in Memoir 26 as a result of our viewpoint and emphasis. Of course, we assume responsibility for any different ideas introduced in the notes.

The second set of notes is a series of illustrations with captions, a preface and references. These illustrations are intended to support a brief general review of depositional models and processes necessary to understand stratal impedance geometries and, hence, the reflection character of seismic sequences and seismic facies. A general knowledge of the geometry and facies composition of depositional systems that fill basins is necessary to appreciate fully the principles of seismic stratigraphic interpretation. Readers can refer to references for further self-study on this subject.

These notes are intended to document the current status of seismic stratigraphy and to share our current ideas with those involved in seismic stratigraphic exploration and with those interested in becoming acquainted with the subject. The notes have been used in a great number of courses and, periodically will continue to be updated. They are not intended to meet editorial requirements for a formal monograph on the subject.

The AAPG kindly permitted reproduction of many illustrations from the Bulletin and Memoir 26. A few illustrations are from other published reports and we gratefully acknowledge these sources. Finally we acknowledge our many colleagues worldwide who have contributed to our understanding of basinal stratigraphy and seismic stratigraphic interpretation.

L. F. Brown, Jr.
W. L. Fisher
Bureau of Economic Geology
The University of Texas at Austin
July, 1980

PRINCIPLES OF SEISMIC STRATIGRAPHIC INTERPRETATION

Interpretation of Depositional Systems and Lithofacies from Seismic Data.

by

L. F. BROWN, Jr.
W. L. FISHER

AUSTIN, TEXAS

1979

SEISMIC-STRATIGRAPHIC INTERPRETATION OF DEPOSITIONAL SYSTEMS AND ITS ROLE IN PETROLEUM EXPLORATION[1]

INTRODUCTION

During the past two decades, petroleum exploration has moved into frontier basins both onshore and offshore. Prospects in these basins have become increasingly deeper and often consist of potential deep-water reservoirs, in addition to more conventional shallow marine clastic and carbonate reservoir facies. By definition, frontier basins lack sufficient well control to permit conventional subsurface facies analysis and mapping. Consequently, the explorationist must extract maximum subsurface information from seismic reflection profiles. Without stratigraphic interpretation of frontier basins, exploration is limited to structural anomalies drilled without benefit of reservoir source or seal discrimination. Hence, concepts and techniques of seismic stratigraphic interpretation have developed to meet this need.

Integration of geophysical data with stratigraphic concepts has added a new dimension to basin analysis. Recent advancements in geophysical data acquisition and processing, coupled with parallel advancements in depositional systems concepts, are responsible for the recent surge of interest in seismic-stratigraphic analysis. Two approaches to seismic stratigraphy have emerged during the last decade: (1) a physical modeling of lithic and fluid composition utilizing computer analysis of velocity, amplitude, frequency, and other wave parame-

---

[1] We wish to acknowledge the significant contributions by Exxon's Vail et al. (1977) to this chapter. Because of proprietary constraints, we have had to rely principally upon their papers for seismic profiles. We have also utilized many ideas, as well as conceptual figures, from their well-structured papers. We assume responsibility for any interpretive or conceptual modifications of their original ideas. Any changes are derived from our own experience in seismic-stratigraphic analysis. In oral presentations, we are able to illustrate presentations with other proprietary seismic examples which cannot be used in this manual.

ters; and (2) a stratigraphic/facies approach using reflection sections and geophysical logs (if available) to interpret lithofacies and, subsequently, depositional systems. Recognition of depositional systems on seismic profiles permits mapping of potential reservoir, source, and seal deposits, and provides the basis for reconstructing the structural, depositional, and erosional history of the basin. A depositional systems approach to seismic stratigraphy permits basin analysis using principally geophysical data.

Geologists generally need to improve their understanding of seismic geophysics and to work closely with geophysical interpreters. On the other hand, geophysicists generally will benefit from review of stratigraphic concepts and newer ideas about facies analysis and depositional processes.

We would like to point out specifically the contribution of the series of papers in American Association of Petroleum Geologists Memoir 26, by P. R. Vail, R. M. Mitchum, R. G. Todd, J. M. Widmer, S. Thompson III, J. B. Sangree, J. N. Bubb, and W. G. Hatlelid of Exxon companies. These papers culminated almost two decades of work in seismic stratigraphy by Exxon and constitute the single authoritative source of published concepts, ideas, techniques, and examples. Readers will note that most examples of seismic profiles and conceptual figures in this chapter are from papers by these Exxon explorationists and are credited to Vail et al. (1977). Because of the proprietary nature of seismic data, we have had to rely principally upon published profiles, and most of them are published Exxon profiles. Related lectures are expanded with proprietary examples that cannot be included in the manual.

Our experience in seismic stratigraphy developed independently during the past eight years from consulting studies for Petrobras (Petroleo Brasileiro S.A.). During the past three years, we also have had the opportunity to review seismic data for several international companies from basins throughout the world. Concepts and methods that we developed (Brown and Fisher, 1977) are essentially the same as those published by Vail et al. (1977). Nomenclatural differences that existed have been subsequently standardized. Variations between our approach and that of Vail et al. (1977) involve differences in interpreting the control of cyclic sequences and the origin of marine onlap. Differences result from subjectivity involved in understanding the respective roles played by eustatic sea level changes and basinal tectonics in controlling relative sea level changes. Opinions are examined later in the chapter.

GEOLOGIC SIGNIFICANCE OF SEISMIC REFLECTIONS

An important fundamental of seismic-stratigraphic interpretation is an understanding of the geologic factors that generate the reflection. Except for fluid contacts (oil/water, gas/water) which may cut across strata, primary seismic reflections are in response to significant impedance (density/velocity) changes along (1) stratal surfaces or (2) unconformities. Stratal surfaces are bedding contacts which represent relict depositional surfaces rather than arbitrarily defined lithostratigraphic boundaries.

Unconformities are surfaces of erosion or non-deposition which represent gaps in the geologic record. Unconformities generate reflections because they commonly separate strata with different physical properties or attitudes. In addition, strata below unconformities are commonly weathered or altered mineralogically, thus providing a density/velocity contrast. Reflections in response to an unconformity are diachronous because the time gap or hiatus generally varies along an unconformity. Even though it is diachronous, all strata below an unconformity are older than all strata above it; thus, strata between unconformities constitute time-stratigraphic units. Unconformities generally occur at an angle to underlying and/or overlying stratal surfaces. An angular unconformity may occur where strata below an unconformity were truncated at an angle by erosion. Strata above an unconformity (either angular or non-angular) may conform to the underlying surface or may have been deposited at an angle to the surface (baselap, downlap, onlap). Where strata above and below the unconformity are parallel (or concordant), the unconformity may be verified by paleontologic or isotopic data or by tracing it laterally until it exhibits discordance with stratal reflections.

Stratal surfaces, on the other hand, represent conformable changes in depositional regime (energy, sedimentation rates, environment) and, hence, are relict depositional surfaces. Because they are depositional surfaces, seismic responses to the stratal surface(s) are chrono-stratigraphic reflections. Reflections will be generated from those surfaces which coincide with a significant change in velocity and density. It should be recognized that not every stratal surface will be represented by a unique reflection, because of resolution limits (depending on wavelength/frequency), phase interference, and other physical constraints. Reflections originating from stratigraphic sequences may represent a single specific stratal surface or the reflection may represent the sum (or average) of several stratal responses. Consequently, the reflection conforms with the collective configurations, continuities, velocity-density contrasts, and other physical properties exhibited by the responding strata.

Vail et al. (1977) list the principal factors or parameters used in seismic-stratigraphic interpretation and their probable geologic significance (fig. 1). They noted that *configuration* of reflections is principally geologic in origin, controlled by bedding patterns that are, in turn, related to depositional processes, original depositional topography/bathymetry, erosion, and later developed fluid contacts. The *continuity* of a reflection depends on the continuity of the density-velocity contrast along the stratal surface(s); continuity of the bedding is directly related to depositional processes/environments. *Amplitude* of the reflection is principally controlled by the degree of velocity-density contrast along stratal surfaces, but optimum bed spacing (relative to frequency) may result in phasing lower energy responses to amplify the reflected energy. Fluid contrasts within the strata also may increase further the normal rock velocity-density. Reflection *frequency* is induced by the seismic energy source and may be modified by bed thickness which controls the spacing of reflectors. Lateral velocity changes due to fluid content and lateral thickness changes will affect frequency. *Interval velocity*, which is a critical factor in seismic data processing, provides information on lithology, porosity, and fluid composition. As we will see later, the external geometry of a group of similar reflections (i.e., seismic facies) provides exceed-

SEISMIC FACIES PARAMETERS	GEOLOGIC INTERPRETATION
REFLECTION CONFIGURATION	• BEDDING PATTERNS • DEPOSITIONAL PROCESSES • EROSION AND PALEOTOPOGRAPHY • FLUID CONTACTS
REFLECTION CONTINUITY	• BEDDING CONTINUITY • DEPOSITIONAL PROCESSES
REFLECTION AMPLITUDE	• VELOCITY-DENSITY CONTRAST • BED SPACING • FLUID CONTENT
REFLECTION FREQUENCY	• BED THICKNESS • FLUID CONTENT
INTERVAL VELOCITY	• ESTIMATION OF LITHOLOGY • ESTIMATION OF POROSITY • FLUID CONTENT
EXTERNAL FORM & AREAL ASSOCIATION OF SEISMIC FACIES UNITS	• GROSS DEPOSITIONAL ENVIRONMENT • SEDIMENT SOURCE • GEOLOGIC SETTING

Figure 1. Seismic reflection parameters used in seismic stratigraphy, and their geologic significance. From Mitchum et al. (1977).

ingly important insight about the lithofacies analogue. Also lateral variations in the character of a reflection or group of reflections may be used to infer facies changes.

There has been a general tendency among geologists and geophysicists to infer that seismic reflections will transgress time lines, and consequently will conform to lithostratigraphic facies. We concur with Vail et al. (1977) that seismic reflections are *isochronous* and cross lithostratigraphic facies boundaries. Consequently, the seismic reflection (excluding unconformities) may pass laterally through a variety of lithofacies. Figure 2 shows a shelf system (right) prograding basinward (left) by sigmoid offlap. Seismic reflections may be traced continuously through the shelf system, over the shelf-edge, and downward through an equivalent slope system. Reflections exhibit high continuity, although changes in their wave-form, frequency, and amplitude occur along the continuous reflection. These changes in reflection character mark the effect on the reflection of transitional facies changes. We have observed this same relationship on scores of seismic lines. Where sufficient well data are available, it is possible to relate the lateral changes in reflection character to lithofacies changes. Consequently, one can trace the facies change on the seismic profile and facies isopach maps may be prepared.

Even discontinuous stratal reflections can be traced with reasonable precision to provide a chronostratigraphic correlation. The reflection may weaken or disappear where stratal surfaces with high velocity-density contrasts (and, therefore, high amplitude reflection) grade laterally into facies with low contrast. Nevertheless, it is generally possible to trace reflections across a variety of equivalent lithofacies, permitting the preparation of a variety of contemporaneous lithofacies maps (if at least limited well control is available to verify the facies composition). Such lithofacies maps may also serve as contemporaneous depositional environment maps. In Brazilian offshore basins we have been able to trace isochronous reflections basinward through contemporaneous fan delta, shelf limestone/shale, limestone shelf edges, and slope clinoforms (Brown and Fisher, 1977). Because of lateral changes in continuity, amplitude, and frequency, we were able to

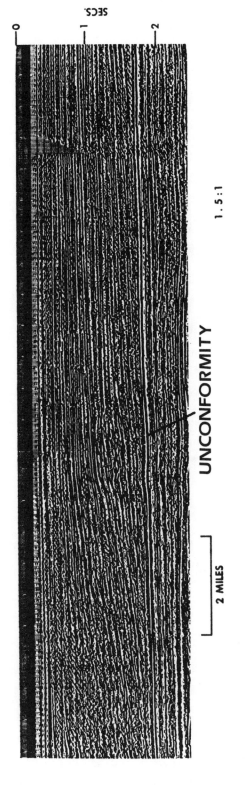

Figure 2. Sigmoid-progradational seismic facies, offshore eastern Canada. From Sangree and Widmier (1977).

calibrate the reflections with lithic data from wells and prepare facies
isopach maps. A similar example (figs. 3, 4) from the San Juan Basin
(Vail et al., 1977) exhibits reflections that can be traced with wavelet
changes through fluvial, deltaic, and prodelta facies. The reader
is referred to additional documentation of the isochronous nature of
stratal reflections by Vail et al. (1977, pp. 100-106), who illustrate
that reflections from Tertiary strata in South America follow stratal
surfaces based on velocity correlation, rather than conventional lithofacies correlation.

SEISMIC REFLECTIONS
AND TIME-STRATIGRAPHY

° A seismic reflection is inferred to represent an isochronous
surface _except_ where the reflection surface is an unconformity identified by toplap, baselap, onlap, or truncation.

° Isochronous reflections may pass through many facies identified by changes in amplitude, frequency, etc. Facies boundaries may be approximated by identifying waveform
changes.

Seismic reflections from stratal surfaces are isochronous. They
provide the basis for chronostratigraphic correlation and for a time-
stratigraphic framework based on seismic profiles. If paleontologic
data are available from wells, time-stratigraphic interpretations can be
correlated throughout the basin. Limited paleontologic control, therefore, can be extrapolated to produce a regional time-stratigraphic framework. Similarly, a hiatus represented by an unconformity can be determined by dating strata above and below each unconformity. Chronostratigraphic representation of strata and hiatuses can be constructed along
each seismic line, permitting graphic illustration of the sequential
history of the basin. Extrapolation and interpretation of seismic data
and paleontologic/lithic information from available wells provide a
comprehensive perspective of basin history with very limited well control.

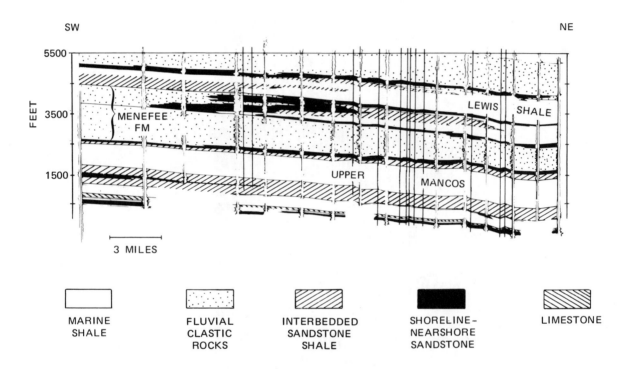

Figure 3. Geologic section based on electric logs from the San Juan basin, New Mexico. From Vail et al. (1977).

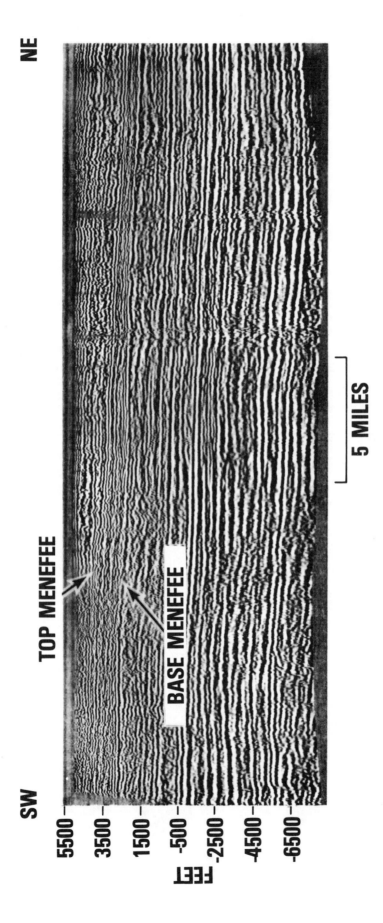

Figure 4. Seismic section connected to depth, San Juan basin, New Mexico. Datum elevation: 5,500 ft (1,676 m). From Vail et al. (1977).

THE SEISMIC STRATIGRAPHIC APPROACH

The seismic-stratigraphic approach permits the explorationist to infer subjective stratigraphic relationships, to interpret depositional processes, and to invoke lithofacies models, in addition to conventional structural mapping. The approach permits interpretation of lithofacies, unconformities, paleobathymetry, isochronous correlations, subsidence and tilting history, facies changes, and general depositional history, among others. In addition, a variety of maps can be generated from seismic data including lithofacies maps, paleobathymetric maps, paleogeographic maps, subcrop maps along unconformities, submarine canyon maps, shelf-edge maps, and a variety of isopach maps of depositional systems, time-stratigraphic units, and stratigraphic facies such as seal and source deposits. Interpretation may be highly subjective, but when conclusions are logical and consistent with known basinal models, they become very useful tools in exploration.

As discussed earlier, seismic reflections (when properly processed) are generated by stratal (depositional) surfaces or unconformities where significant velocity/density contrast exists. Consequently, the attitude, continuity, pinchout, lapout, or truncation of reflections permit the interpreter to use the seismic profile to infer superposition, depositional topography, erosion, non-deposition, and other stratigraphic aspects. The chronostratigraphic nature of stratal surfaces (depositional topography) that generate reflections permits time-stratigraphic correlations on the seismic profile and calibration of the reflections with paleontologic or isotopic data.

By trial and error, most explorationists attempting to interpret the stratigraphic significance of a reflection profile have generally developed similar approaches and procedures. Vail et al. (1977) have graphically illustrated their procedures (fig. 1). We described similar procedures (Brown and Fisher, 1977) based on Brazilian offshore studies.

A procedure called *seismic sequence analysis* (fig. 1) involves recognition of principal reflection packages called seismic sequences. Seismic sequence analysis, which will be discussed and illustrated later, involves delineation of fundamental depositional (stratigraphic) units,

called depositional sequences by Vail et al. (1977), which are bounded
by unconformities or equivalent conformities. Correlation of sequences
throughout the seismic grid, followed by isopach mapping of the
sequence using selected shot-point control, is a first step in
sequence analysis. Basin-wide sequences provide a first-order time-
stratigraphic framework for the region.

The next step in seismic stratigraphic analysis is conversion of
geophysical and core/sample well data from *depth to time* (fig. 5). Time
plots can be placed directly on the seismic profile to provide lithic
and other rock properties with which to interpret seismic facies.

Seismic facies analysis (fig. 5) is a critical part of the interpretation program. It involves recognition of lesser reflection units
within a sequence which may be the seismic response to a lithofacies.
Seismic facies are characterized by reflections displaying distinctive
reflection continuity, amplitude and frequencies, external geometry,
perhaps interval velocity, as well as reflection configuration. Seismic
facies reflections may terminate abruptly or grade into those of other
seismic facies. Mapping of the seismic facies at maximum shot-point
control is an important part of the analyses because external geometry
generally aids in interpretation of the corresponding lithofacies.

Reflection character analysis of the individual reflections permits
more sophisticated interpretation of the seismic facies by analysis of
wave form, amplitude, and frequency, among others. Such analysis carried
out by a geophysicist may serve to verify the seismic facies interpretation.

Final *geologic interpretation* (fig. 5) involves integration and interpretation of seismic sequence and facies analysis in order to map
and chart paleogeography and geologic history, respectively. Maps and
cross sections may be converted from time to depth at this stage. The
distribution of inferred depositional system(s) within each sequence
aids in recognition and mapping of facies boundaries, shelf edges, and
other major stratigraphic features.

Play and prospect evaluation (fig. 5) is the application of ac-
quired seismic stratigraphic data in order to define, map, and evaluate
potential reservoirs, source beds, and seals for structural and

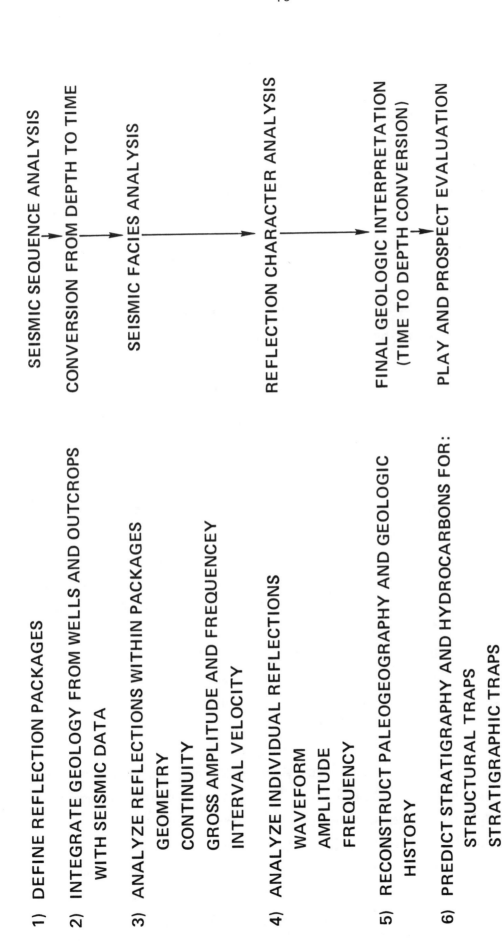

1) DEFINE REFLECTION PACKAGES

2) INTEGRATE GEOLOGY FROM WELLS AND OUTCROPS
   WITH SEISMIC DATA

3) ANALYZE REFLECTIONS WITHIN PACKAGES
   GEOMETRY
   CONTINUITY
   GROSS AMPLITUDE AND FREQUENCEY
   INTERVAL VELOCITY

4) ANALYZE INDIVIDUAL REFLECTIONS
   WAVEFORM
   AMPLITUDE
   FREQUENCY

5) RECONSTRUCT PALEOGEOGRAPHY AND GEOLOGIC
   HISTORY

6) PREDICT STRATIGRAPHY AND HYDROCARBONS FOR:
   STRUCTURAL TRAPS
   STRATIGRAPHIC TRAPS

SEISMIC SEQUENCE ANALYSIS

CONVERSION FROM DEPTH TO TIME

SEISMIC FACIES ANALYSIS

REFLECTION CHARACTER ANALYSIS

FINAL GEOLOGIC INTERPRETATION
(TIME TO DEPTH CONVERSION)

PLAY AND PROSPECT EVALUATION

Figure 5. Procedures followed by Exxon explorationists during a seismic-stratigraphic interpretation. From Vail et al. (1976). AAPG Seismic Stratigraphy course notes.

stratigraphic traps. Success of this phase depends principally upon
the experience and perspective of the explorationist. Inferred geologic scenarios (deposition, submarine erosion, subaerial exposure/
erosion, structural conditions, among others) for each sequence provide
the tools to outline potential prospects. Conceptually the process
differs very little from conventional prospecting except that seismically
derived stratigraphic data are applied. Innovative maps are important
at this stage to integrate all pertinent prospect elements.

RECOGNITION AND DISCRIMINATION
OF DEPOSITIONAL SEQUENCES

Geologists have long recognized the presence of major depositional
sequences composed of genetically related facies or depositional systems.
Dramatic examples of depositional sequences are those exhibiting clinoforms (figs. 6, 7). Figure 6 illustrates Carboniferous progradational
slope shale and sandstone clinoforms in West Texas that were periodically
interrupted by deposition of shelf/slope limestones. The base of these
depositional sequences is marked by downward convergence and pinchout
(baselap/downlap) of slope clinoforms. Some deep-water sandstones (submarine fans) at the base of the clinoforms appear to onlap the toe of
the slope. Clinoform limestones can be traced up the slope and into
widespread shelf limestones. Studies by Galloway and Brown (1973) show
that slope sandstone and shale clinoforms terminate abruptly (toplap)
at the base of delta-front sandstones within shelf-margin delta systems.
Cretaceous examples from the U.S. Western Interior basin (Asquith,
1970) show similar depositional sequences (fig. 7). Prograding delta
systems supplied clastic sediment to slope/basin environments resulting
in pronounced clinoforms delineated by correlation of bentonitic clays
in closely spaced wells. Vail et al. (1977) show a similar example
defined by densely spaced geophysical log correlations. Seismic response to depositional sequences such as those shown by figures 6 and
7 generally resemble the seismic section in figure 8. One can easily
translate mentally from the stratigraphic cross section to the seismic
profile. The seismic profile shows clearly that the younger part of

15

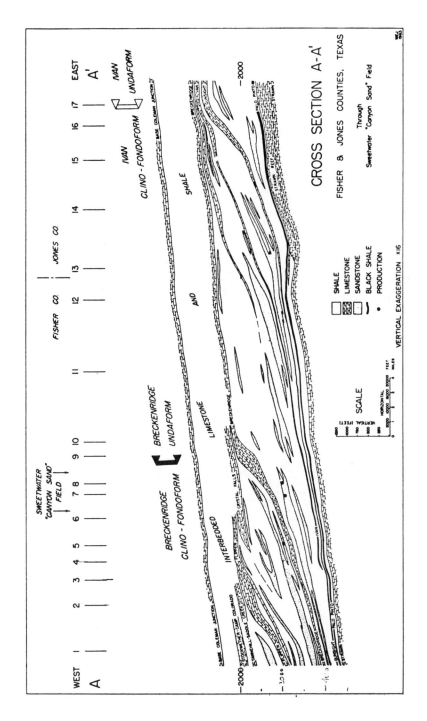

Figure 6. Slope facies displayed by successive prograding Cisco depositional sequences, Eastern Shelf, North-central Texas. From Jackson (1964).

16

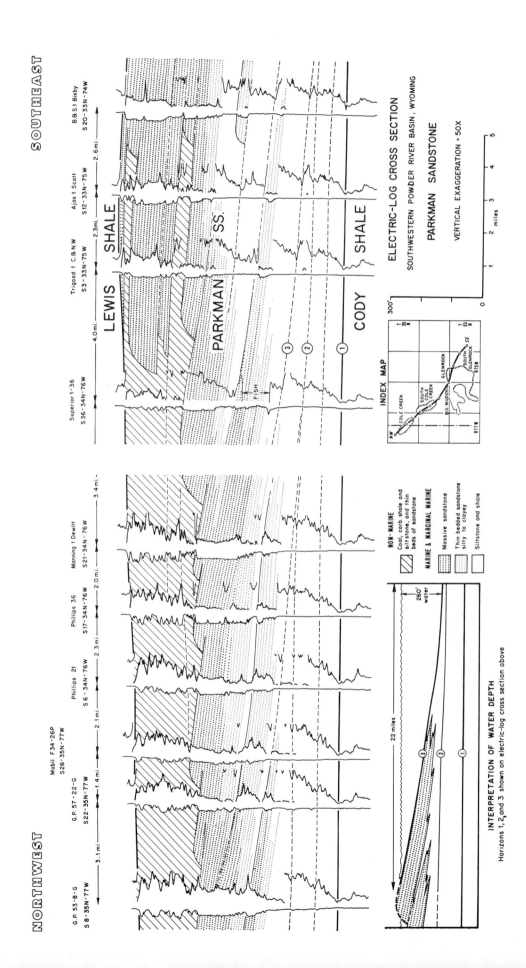

SOUTHEAST

NORTHWEST

ELECTRIC-LOG CROSS SECTION
SOUTHWESTERN POWDER RIVER BASIN, WYOMING
PARKMAN SANDSTONE
VERTICAL EXAGGERATION = 50X

LEWIS SHALE
PARKMAN SS.
CODY SHALE

INDEX MAP

NON-MARINE
Coal, carb shale and siltstone, and thin beds of sandstone

MARINE & MARGINAL MARINE
Massive sandstone
Thin bedded sandstone silty to clayey
Siltstone and shale

INTERPRETATION OF WATER DEPTH
Horizons 1, 2, and 3 shown on electric-log cross section above

Figure 7. Electric log cross section, regressive (prograding) part of Lewis Shale, Fox Hills Sandstone, and lower Lance Formation, Washakie and Red Desert basins, Wyoming. From Asquith (1970).

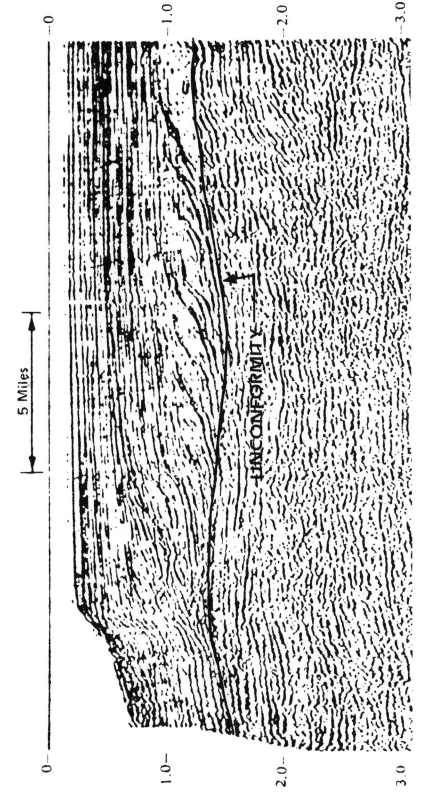

Figure 8. Progradation of a shelf-margin delta system. Proprietary section of United Geophysical Corporation. From Dobrin (1977).

the basin-fill was deposited by rapidly prograding delta/slope systems
(oblique clinoforms) which gave way to slowly prograding shelf/slope
systems (sigmoid clinoforms). Continuous, high amplitude clinoform
reflections represent periodic deposition of hemipelagic suspension
sediments; poorly defined to reflector-free clinoforms were deposited
more rapidly by density-transported clastics introduced into deep water
by shelf-margin deltas (oblique) and later by tidal currents (sigmoid).

By recognizing principal unconformities within the sedimentary fill
of a basin, the interpreter may subdivide the strata into genetic units
or *depositional sequences* that approximate the scale (thickness and
time) of time-stratigraphic series. Seismic resolution generally pre-
cludes recognition of minor genetic units, but normally permits resolution of sequences composed of major depositional systems--e.g.,
delta/slope, carbonate platform/slope, or thick continental rise (marine
onlap) systems. Vail et al. (1977) illustrated the delineation of
seismic sequences from offshore Northwest Africa (fig. 9). Readers can
refer to their reports (idem., pp. 145-163) for a seismic-stratigraphic
analysis of the area. On figure 9 one can recognize regional unconformities, angular, non-angular,and lapouts, which separate the
depositional sequences. Age of the sequences, based on well control,
shows the approximate magnitude of the fundamental depositional sequences. Arrows illustrate reflection terminations--erosional and
lapouts (onlap, toplap, and downlap/baselap). In general, a cursory
review of the African line and well data shows that (1) a Jurassic
shelf/platform (probably carbonates and mixed fine-grained clastics)
was established over earlier rift-related Triassic red beds and relict
rift structures followed by marine onlap; (2) Early Cretaceous delta
systems prograded across the shelf and into deep water over a contemporaneous slope system accompanied by synsedimentary faulting; (3) a Late
Cretaceous onlap shelf system; and (4) Tertiary alternating offlap and
onlap slope systems. Considerable speculation about the lithofacies can
be made, even without well control, by recognizing the depositional
systems that were operative in the basin following rifting.

Terms introduced by Vail et al. (1977) are descriptive of unconformities bounding depositional sequences (fig. 10). These terms

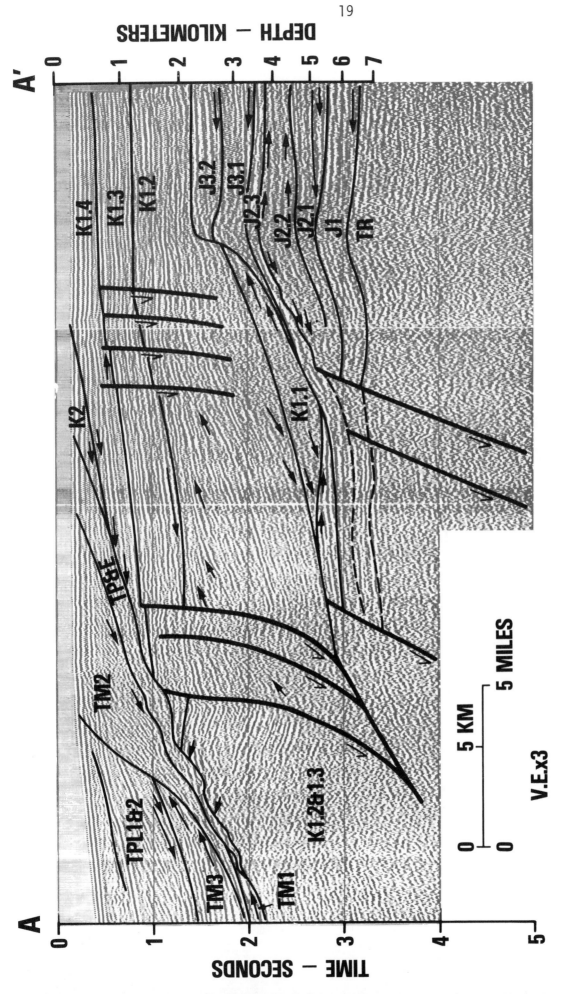

Figure 9. Seismic sequences from offshore northwest Africa showing sequences defined by seismic reflections. From Mitchum et al. (1977).

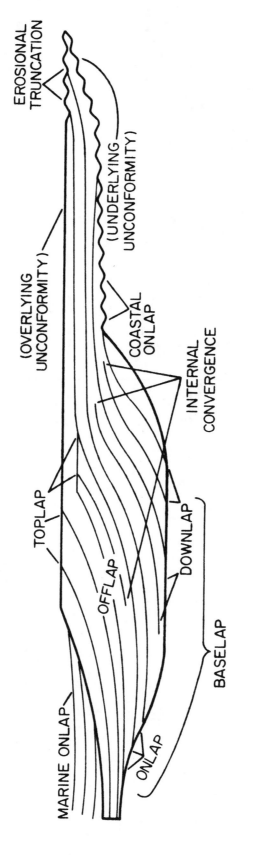

Figure 10. Terminology proposed by Exxon explorationists for reflection terminations that define unconformable boundaries of a depositional sequence. From Vail et al. (1976), AAPG Seismic Stratigraphy course notes.

are generally self-explanatory. Lapout terms--toplap, onlap, and down-lap--describe reflection terminations produced by depositional processes. If onlap or downlap cannot be verified because of subsequent structural effects, baselap is used to define the basal termination. Toplap is widespread and constitutes a sequence boundary, but it may be localized and occur within a sequence. Marine onlap may occur basinward and distal to prograding clinoforms (distal marine onlap) or it may occur shelfward and proximal to prograding clinoforms (proximal onlap). Land-ward onlap of shallow marine coastal deposits (deltas, barrier bars, etc.) is called coastal onlap.

Erosional unconformities may be recognized by truncation (termina-tion) of underlying strata. Angular unconformities of tilted strata are common, but not restricted, to landward margins of basins where progressive uplift and erosion is common. Submarine erosion of outer shelf and slope strata generally results in truncation of reflections arranged in normal depositional attitudes. We have observed submarine canyons that have eroded up to 2,500 meters into shelf/slope sediments.

BOUNDARIES OF
DEPOSITIONAL SEQUENCES

- ° Erosional boundaries
- ° Lapout (hiatal) boundaries
- ° Conformable boundaries (rare)

The significance of unconformities bounding sequences can be evalu-ated by the type(s) of termination (erosional or lapouts) and the dis-cordant attitude(s) of reflections above and/or below the unconformity. The hiatus represented by an unconformity generally varies throughout its extent. Magnitude of an angular unconformity increases in the direction of older eroded strata. Magnitude of a baselap unconformity increases in the direction of lapout. Magnitude of a toplap unconformity increases opposite to the direction of progradation. Unconformities recognized by truncation and/or lapouts generally can be traced into concordant reflections, where evidence of an unconformity can be verified only by paleontologic or isotopic age determinations above and below the concordant sequence boundary. There are areas in most basins where such concordant sequence boundaries may, in fact, be conformable.

In summary, depositional sequences are composed of genetically related strata deposited by one or more contemporaneous depositional systems. Sequences are bounded by unconformities characterized by both discordant and concordant reflections; discordant reflections may be either erosional (truncated) or depositional (lapouts). The depositional sequence is the preserved record of a major episode of deposition within a basin and, consequently, constitutes a principal chapter in the history of the basin (fig. 11).

DEPOSITIONAL SEQUENCE

° A *depositional sequence* is a stratigraphic unit composed of a relatively conformable succession of genetically related strata.

° The upper and lower *boundaries* of a depositional sequence are unconformities or their correlative conformable surfaces.

The depositional sequence is a major genetic unit within a basin, and because it is bounded by unconformities, it constitutes a time-stratigraphic unit. Consequently, all strata within the sequence were deposited during a given interval of time (fig. 12). Internally, the strata are generally conformable and are genetically related to a major depositional episode. A variety of facies compose a sequence, but isochronous stratal reflections pass laterally through various lithofacies. It is this genetic, time-stratigraphic aspect of seismic sequences that make them important in basin analysis.

Basins are filled by superposed depositional sequences, commonly arranged in cycles of offlapping and onlapping marine strata and related onlapping coastal strata. Variations in relative sea level, controlled by the interplay of eustatic sea level changes and variable rates of basin subsidence and tilting and variable rates of sedimentation are

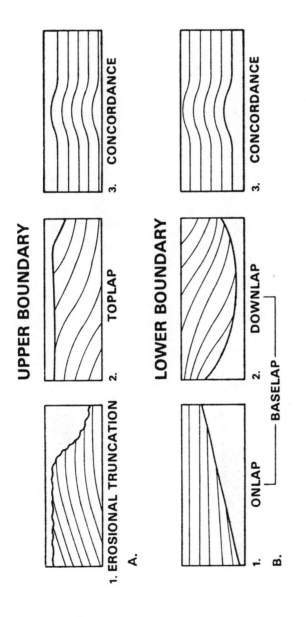

Figure 11. Various relationships of strata to depositional sequence boundaries. From Mitchum et al. (1977).

24

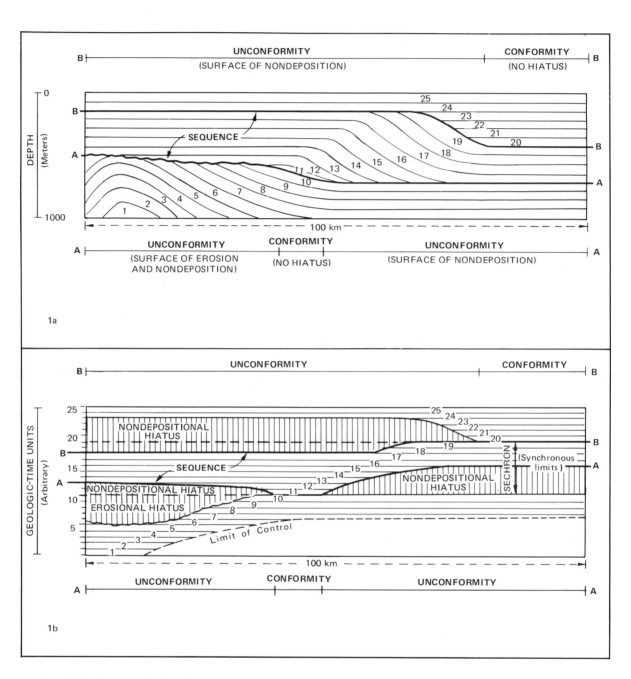

Figure 12. Basic concepts of a depositional sequence. (A) Generalized stratigraphic section of a sequence. (B) Generalized chronostratigraphic section of a sequence. From Mitchum et al. (1977).

inferred to control cyclic deposition. Control of cyclic seismic sequences will be reviewed later in this chapter.

Once a depositional sequence has been recognized on one or more reflection profiles, bounding unconformities may be traced along available seismic profiles. Bounding unconformities must tie along all correlation loops throughout the grid. Geophysical well, core, or sample data should be plotted on the time section. In addition, we believe that at this time the interpreter should construct travel-time (or depth) isopach maps of each depositional sequence. The map defines external geometry and distribution of each principal genetic unit in the basin and serves as the time-stratigraphic framework for subsequent seismic facies analysis.

STRATIGRAPHIC INTERPRETATION
OF SEISMIC FACIES

The stage is set for more detailed seismic facies analysis (Vail et al., 1977) when the interpreter has completed the seismic sequence analysis.

FACTORS FOR INTERPRETING
SEISMIC FACIES

° Internal reflection composition and configuration:

   ° Continuity
   ° Amplitude/frequency
   ° Interval velocity

° Boundary relationships

   ° Termination(al)
   ° Transitional

° External geometry

° Lateral facies relationships

Seismic facies analysis first involves recognition of distinctive "packages" of reflections within each sequence. Each package of reflections differs in some respect from other surrounding reflections, thus constituting anomalous reflections on the profile. More specifically, each reflection package exhibits a combination of physical characteristics that distinguish it from adjacent seismic facies. Distinguishing factors include (1) reflection configuration, (2) reflection continuity, (3) reflection amplitude and frequency, (4) bounding relationships, i.e., types(s) of reflection termination or lateral change, (5) interval velocity, and (6) external geometry of the reflection package. Except for interval velocity and external geometry, these factors can be evaluated visually on the seismic profile. Computer processing techniques, however, may be used to emphasize or exaggerate seismic facies properties. Research in this area can enhance characteristics that are most important in seismic facies analysis. Estimation of interval velocity can be supplied by the geophysical processor and external geometry can be mapped by the interpreter.

Seismic facies mapping can be carried out using time or thickness values determined and plotted at closely spaced shot-points. In delineating seismic facies for mapping purposes, some degree of subjectivity is generally involved. Boundaries of the seismic facies may be sharp, easily recognized erosional or lapout boundaries. However, in other cases boundaries may be abruptly or gradually transitional. Transitional boundaries may be selected arbitrarily where composition of individual reflections change laterally in amplitude, continuity, frequency and/or cycle breadth. Lateral changes in bed thickness, related to a lithofacies change, may also result in termination of reflections at the seismic facies boundary; this has been called internal convergence (fig. 10).

DEFINITION OF SEISMIC FACIES

° A seismic facies is an areally definable,
  3-dimensional unit composed of seismic
  reflections whose elements, such as
  reflection configuration, amplitude, continuity, frequency, and interval velocity,
  differ from the elements of adjacent facies
  units.

° A seismic facies unit is interpreted to
  express certain lithology, stratification,
  and depositional features of the deposits
  that generate the reflections in the unit.

A fundamental precept in seismic facies analysis is that a seismic
facies is the sonic response to a lithofacies. Reflections within
seismic facies, therefore, are inferred to represent stratal surfaces,
unconformities of stratigraphic significance, or possibly fluid contacts.
If processing of the data has been accomplished with a high degree of
precision, the explorationist may cautiously view the profile as a
"sonic picture" of subsurface stratigraphy. Seismic facies, therefore,
provide the interpreter with a variety of information useful for determining the lithostratigraphic analogue. Seismic facies analysis is
most successful when sufficient profiles are available to place the
facies within the regional context of a depositional sequence. Nevertheless, some stratigraphic interpretation is generally possible even
with limited geographic coverage.

In general, stratigraphic interpretation of seismic facies may be
viewed as a process of elimination. For example, the interpreter may
immediately eliminate a number of lithofacies/depositional environments
because of obvious inconsistencies with available data and/or personal
knowledge of the basin. Several alternative stratigraphic interpretations may remain viable. Further analysis will generally reduce the
options further. A final, conclusive interpretation may not be possible
and the best interpretation may be one that is most compatible with

available data.

Principal Types of Seismic Facies

Lithofacies interpretation of seismic facies involves consideration of internal reflection configurations, boundary relationships, lateral facies relationships, and external geometry. For convenience, we will review each principal type of reflection configuration, including consideration of associated geometry, lateral facies equivalents, and boundary reflectionships. This approach follows methodology of Vail et al. (1977) with certain modifications.

PRINCIPAL TYPES OF SEISMIC REFLECTION CONFIGURATIONS

- ° Parallel/divergent
- ° Progradational
- ° Mounded/draped
- ° Onlap/fills

With limited experience, one can recognize the principal types of classes of reflection configurations (fig. 13) and bounding relationships (figs. 11, 14). External geometry (fig. 15) can be inferred very accurately with increasing experience, but mapping is required for confirmation. With more experience, the interpreter can begin to predict laterally equivalent seismic facies. Lithogenetic interpretation of seismic facies depends on the interpreter's understanding of depositional processes, lithofacies composition, geometry, and spatial boundary conditions. Seismic facies interpretation is more subjective than lithofacies interpretation. Consequently, conventional basinal analysis experience is highly desirable before undertaking stratigraphic interpretation from seismic reflection data. For this reason, we have preceded this discussion with a review of principal depositional systems and facies. The interpreter will now be required to think "depositionally" but without benefit of adequate lithostratigraphic data.

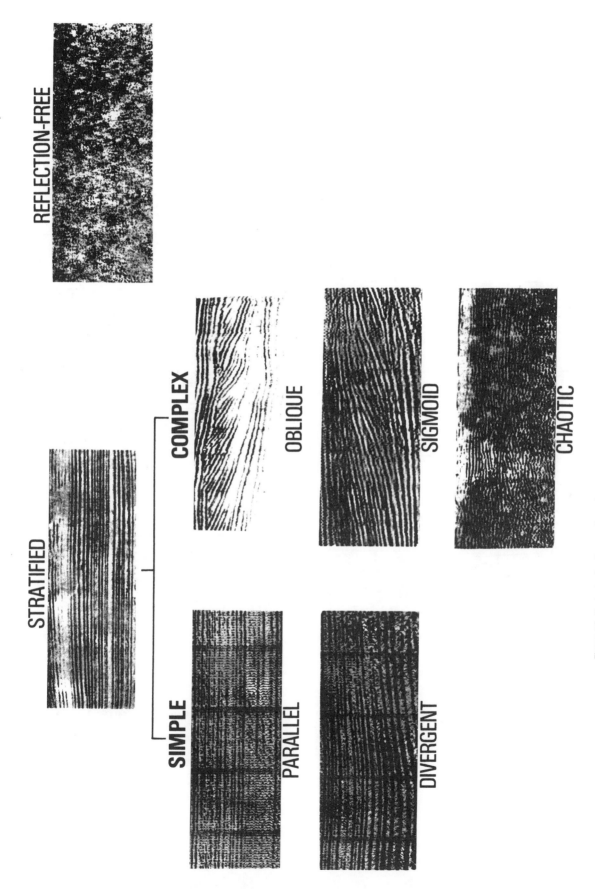

Figure 13. Typical reflection configurations. From Vail et al. (1976), AAPG Seismic Stratigraphy course notes.

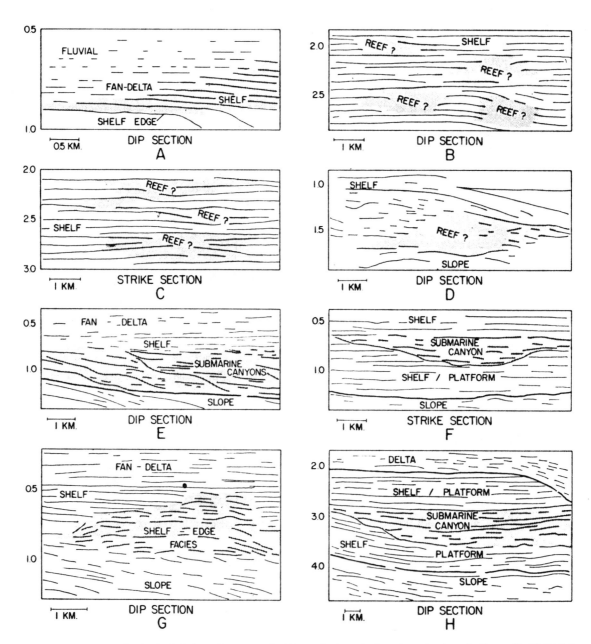

Figure 14. Shelf and associated seismic facies patterns generalized from reflection seismic sections showing reflection configurations and continuity. From Brown and Fisher (1977).

31

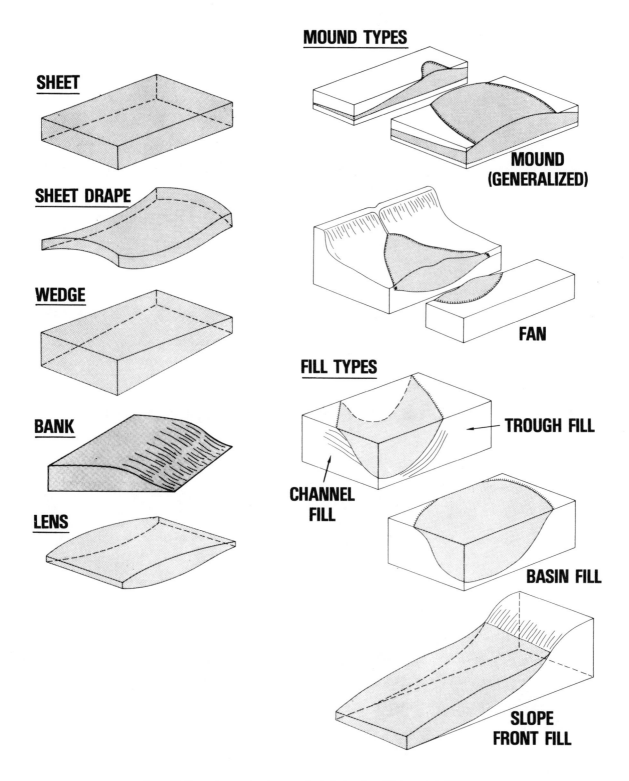

Figure 15. External geometry of some seismic facies. From Mitchum et al. (1977).

The following types of seismic facies are outlined: (1) parallel/ divergent, (2) progradational, (3) mounded/draped, and (4) onlap/fills. The facies name implies the most distinctive and significant aspect of the facies: reflection configuration, bounding relationships, or geometry.

Parallel/Divergent Configurations

Perhaps the most common reflections within basins are parallel or subparallel to divergent in configuration (fig. 16). Amplitude and continuity of this reflection pattern, however, may be quite variable. Generally, these seismic facies are areally extensive.

SEISMIC FACIES TYPES

Parallel/divergent configurations

° High amplitude/high continuity
° Low to moderate amplitude and continuity
° Variable amplitude/low continuity

Because of wide, relatively uniform lateral extent in most basins, it can be inferred that these facies were deposited on a broad, relatively stable shelf, delta platform or, less likely, on a broad basinal plain. These two paleographic settings, shelf and basinal plain, each exhibit widespread, relatively uniform depositional environments. Lithologically, however, these environments are characterized by significantly different lithofacies. Shelf/platform facies consist of neritic shale and/or limestone strata; sandstone is rare and generally transgressive. Delta platform facies consist of shallow-water, high-energy marine (delta-front) sandstone and shale and delta plain shale, channel-fill sandstones, widespread coal or lignite beds, and perhaps thin, calcareous, marine-transgressive sandstone or shale. Shelf/platform and delta platform facies are undaform deposits (Rich, 1952). Basinal plain facies are composed of hemipelagic shale, siltstone, or calcareous clays, commonly arranged in repetitive sequences. They are fondoform deposits according to Rich's terminology. Recognition of basinal plain depositional settings is improved if there is indication of mounded or draped patterns within or immediately below this seismic facies (see later

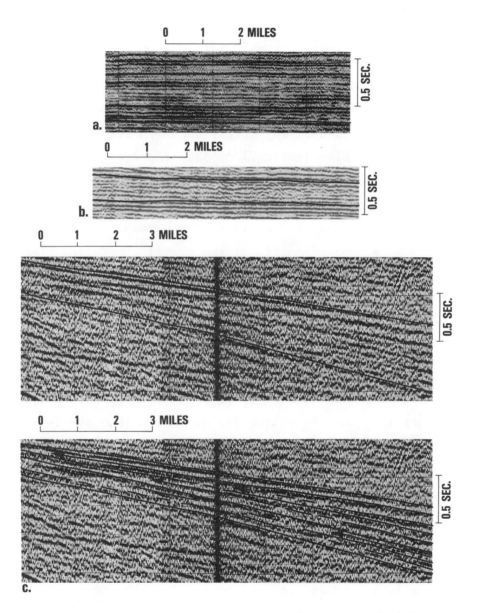

Figure 16. Parallel, subparallel, and divergent seismic reflection configurations. Modified from Mitchum et al. (1977).

discussion of mounded/draped patterns).

Geometry of shelf, delta platform (on a continental shelf), and basinal plain facies is normally tabular, sheet, or wedge-shaped. Beyond a subjacent shelf edge, however, delta systems exhibit significant changes in geometry, reflection configuration, and thickness (fig. 17). On roll-over anticlines delta-front sandstones/shales exhibit a marked divergence in reflections toward contemporaneous growth faults. Divergence of reflections is not unique to delta-front/prodelta facies. Similar seismic facies also may rarely occur in shelf/platform limestone/ shale successions. Divergent reflections, therefore, connote differential rates of subsidence and/or contemporaneous fault movement. On a shelf, delta facies are generally sheet or tabular in geometry. Because of differential sand/shale compaction, it may be possible to observe subtle mounding of delta reflections in strike profiles. Deltaic facies (in strike sections) are the only mounded clastic deposits on a shelf that may be sufficiently thick to be resolved by normal seismic methods.

Another way to distinguish among shelf, delta platform, and basinal plain facies involves recognition of bounding relationships with other seismic facies. It may be possible to trace parallel/divergent facies laterally into more diagnostic facies or into an unconformity. Shelf facies generally grade transitionally basinward into shelf-margin facies and ultimately clinoform progradational slope facies. Basinal plain facies commonly grade shelfward into mounded and/or clinoform facies, or they may onlap truncated progradational reflections (e.g., continental rise onlap). Shelf platform or delta platform (delta-front/delta-plain facies) reflections normally overlie clinoform or progradational reflections--sigmoid (fig. 3) or oblique (fig. 11). Basinal plain seismic facies normally are concordant at the base or they may overlie eroded, mounded seismic facies. Shelf and delta platform seismic facies may be eroded and onlapped by coastal deposits in updip areas (angular unconformity) and in downdip areas these facies may have been eroded by submarine canyons and filled by onlap facies.

Internal configurations of parallel/divergent seismic facies generally are not sufficiently unique to permit differentiation. If the interpreter can eliminate basinal plain facies from consideration (by recognizing mounded/draped configurations or marine onlap), then it is possible to discriminate between shelf/platform and delta platform facies with some reliability. Although both of these seismic facies normally overlie progradational slope facies, slope deposits beneath a delta system (on a shelf) commonly exhibit toplap (oblique offlap). Delta systems that prograded into deep water (e.g., beyond a subjacent shelf edge) normally exhibit well-defined contemporaneous growth faults and roll-over anticlines (figs. 9, 17). On the other hand, slope facies beneath prograding shelf/platform facies (fig. 3) rarely exhibit growth faults and generally exhibit sigmoid progradational facies.

Without regional seismic profiles, the interpreter may be required to consider more subtle variations in reflection configuration (i.e., continuity and amplitude) in order to discriminate between shelf/platform and delta platform facies. A widespread succession of parallel reflections displaying broad cycles of *high amplitude and high continuity* points to a shelf/platform sequence composed of alternating neritic limestones and shales (figs. 9, 18, 19). Uniform reflections characterized this widespread, tectonically stable depositional setting.

High amplitude, parallel/divergent reflections, however, may also be generated by impedance changes between delta-front sandstones and intercalated prodelta shales (figs. 5, 17, 18, 19). Coal or lignite beds and thin, calcareous marine transgressive beds may produce high amplitude reflections in a delta plain succession (figs. 11, 18, 19). High amplitude reflections of the delta platform generally are less continuous and may exhibit narrower cycle breadth (frequency) than those of shelf/platform limestones and shales. More diagnostic of delta platform facies, however, may be the high percentage of reflections with *low to moderate amplitude/continuity*. Deposition within shifting and prograding delta-front environments produces a zone of high amplitude reflections at the base of a delta platform (fig. 19), but continuity of reflections from these imbricate sandstone/shale bodies is generally low to moderate, compared with widespread neritic limestone/shale shelf deposits. Coal/lignite and thin marine transgressive units which may display high continuity/amplitude reflections, normally occur intercalated within low to moderate continuity/amplitude delta plain reflec-

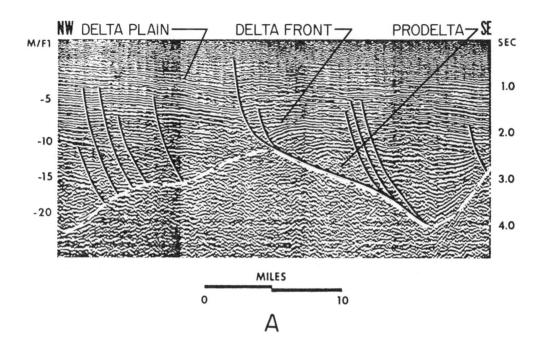

A

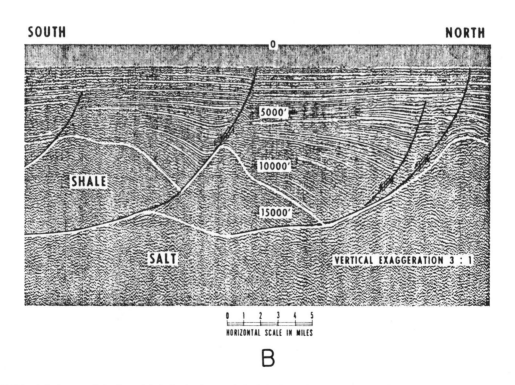

B

Figure 17. Seismic facies, growth faults, and shale diapirs characteristic of shelf-margin delta systems. (A) Tertiary delta systems of the Texas Gulf Coast basin. After Bruce (1973). (B) Plio-Pleistocene delta system Northern Gulf Coast basin. After Woodbury (1973).

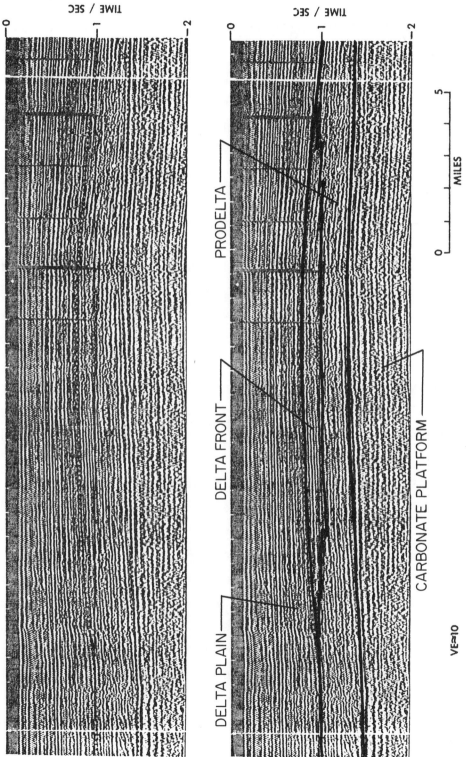

TIME / SEC

TIME / SEC

PRODELTA

DELTA FRONT

CARBONATE PLATFORM

DELTA PLAIN

MILES

VE≃10

Figure 18. Strike seismic profile of a Lower Cretaceous shelf delta system showing broad mound seismic facies, offshore Africa. From Sangree and Widmier (1977).

tions (fig. 19). High amplitude/low to moderate continuity reflections
of the delta front generally grade basinward into narrower cycles of
low/amplitude/low to moderate continuity prodelta facies. Prodelta facies
are normally progradational and may toplap at the base of the parallel/
divergent delta platform reflections (fig. 19). However, if water was
very shallow, prodelta reflections will be continuous updip with delta
front reflections (fig. 5). Where a delta system has prograded beyond
a shelf edge into very deep water, divergent reflections (fig. 17), as
well as internally convergent reflections (fig. 10), coincide with
thickening of beds toward contemporaneous faults and pinch-out of sandstones away from the faults. High amplitude reflections (intercalated
delta-front sandstone/prodelta shales) normally grade basinward into
narrower cycles of low/moderate amplitude reflections (intercalated
prodelta shale/siltstone).

A third variety of parallel/divergent seismic facies are *variable
amplitude/low continuity* reflections. These reflections commonly occur
in response to upper delta plain and alluvial plain facies composed
of high-energy fluvial channels/meanderbelts and low energy flood basin
facies (figs. 17, 19). This configuration also characterizes distal
fan-delta facies which grade updip into reflection-free, proximal fan-
delta sandstone facies (Brown and Fisher, 1977).

In summary, parallel/divergent reflections (figs. 20, 21) are among
the most difficult to interpret because they do not represent unique
depositional settings. Consequently, seismic-stratigraphic interpretation must integrate all available data. Lateral equivalents and
boundary relationships (basal and top) are very important. Careful interpretation of amplitude, continuity, and frequency can be helpful, but
combinations of these parameters are not necessarily exclusive. Figure
22 diagrammatically illustrates some combinations of the reflection
parameters. The following table, modified from one by Vail et al. (1977,
pp. 166-168), summarizes key factors involved in determining depositional
environment (and inferred lithofacies) represented by various parallel/
divergent configurations (table 1).

39

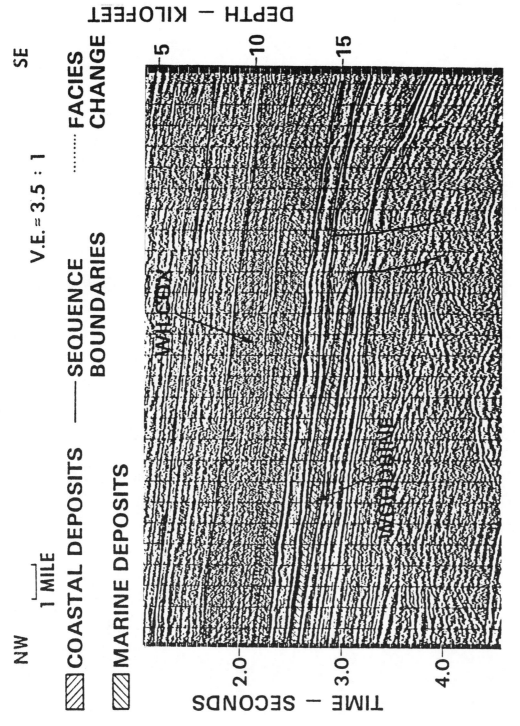

Figure 19. Seismic profile, East Texas. From Vail et al. (1976), AAPG Seismic Stratigraphy course notes.

Progradational Configurations

This general type of seismic facies is probably the easiest to recognize on seismic profiles. In dip sections reflections are inclined relative to underlying and overlying reflections (figs. 3, 8, 9, 13, 19) and have been called offlap reflections (fig. 10) or clinoform reflections (Rich, 1951). This facies is in response to lithofacies deposited within prodelta and/or slope environments during basinward shifting of shelf/platform or delta systems. The process is called progradation. Environments are characterized by inclined depositional surfaces that may range from 0.5° to 15°, although average Holocene slopes of the world are about 4° to 5° (Emery, 1968).

Prodelta facies consist of clay and silt deposited from suspension in front of the prograding delta platform. On a shallow shelf, prodelta facies may grade basinward into shelf facies. Prodelta suspension deposition is generally restricted to water depths above 200-300 ft (60-100 m) even on major deltas. When prodelta sediments are deposited in basins deeper than a few hundred feet, the deeper prodelta deposits are progressively reworked into deeper water by slumping and density flow to produce contemporaneous slope facies. Upper and mid-slope lithofacies are composed of clay or silt-sized clastic or calcareous sediments deposited from suspension. Lower slope facies are typically composed of sand, silt, and clay deposited on submarine fans. A submarine fan is deposited from density or turbidity flows that decrease velocity because of lower gradients at the base of the slope.

A variety of progradational configurations are possible, but two fundamental types are called oblique and sigmoid (fig. 23). They may occur in the same progradational system, reflecting changes in relative sea-level and/or depositional rates. Other variations such as shingled configurations are also common (fig. 24).

SEISMIC FACIES TYPES

Progradational configurations
- ° Oblique
- ° Sigmoid
- ° Shingled
- ° Complex/composites

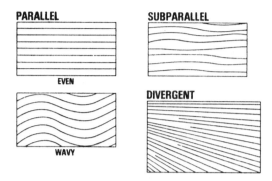

Figure 20. Parallel, subparallel and divergent seismic reflection configurations. From Mitchum et al. (1977).

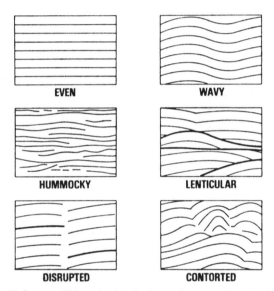

Figure 21. Some modifying seismic reflection configurations. From Mitchum et al. (1977).

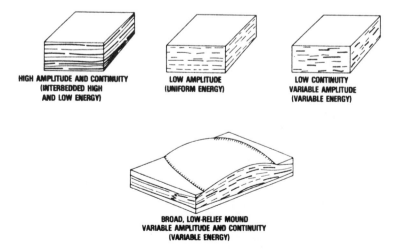

Figure 22. Diagrammatic illustration of shelf and shelf-data seismic facies. From Sangree and Widmier (1977).

Table 1. Summary of seismic facies characterized by parallel and divergent reflection configurations*

Properties of Seismic Facies	Depositional Environments/Settings			
	Shelf/Platform	Delta Platform: *delta front/delta plain*	Alluvial Plain/ Distal Fan Delta	Basinal Plain
Reflection configuration	Parallel/slightly divergent; highly divergent near rare growth faults	Parallel/slightly divergent on shelf; highly divergent near growth faults in deep-water deltas	Parallel, generally grades basinward into delta plain or into shelf/ platform facies	Parallel/slightly divergent; may grade laterally into divergent fills or mounds
Lithofacies and composition	Alternating neritic limestone and shale; rare sandstone; undaform deposits	Shallow marine delta front sandstone/shale grading upward into subaerial delta plain shale, coal, sandstone channels; prodelta facies excluded except where toplap is absent; undaform deposits	Meanderbelt and channel-fill sandstone and floodbasin mudstone; marine reworked fan delta sandstones/ profan shale; undaform deposits	Alternating hemipelagic clays and siltstone; calcareous and terrigenous composition; fondoform deposits
Geometry and structure	Sheet-like to wedge shaped or tabular; very stable setting; uniform subsidence	Sheet-like to wedge shaped or tabular on shelf- prismatic to lenticular basinward of subjacent shelf edge with growth faults and roll-over anticlines; relatively stable, uniform subsidence on shelf; rapid subsidence and faulting in deep-water delta	Sheet-like to wedge shaped (individually elongate ribbons or lobes), commonly tilted and eroded	Sheet-like to wedge shaped; may be slightly wavy or draped over subjacent mounds; generally stable to uniform subsidence; may grade laterally into active structural areas
Lateral relationships	May grade landward into coastal facies and basinward into shelf-margin carbonate facies; local carbonate mounds	May grade landward into alluvial systems and basinward into prodelta/slope clinoforms (on shelf) or growth-faulted prodelta/slope facies (deep-water setting)	Grade landward into reflection-free, high sandstone facies; alluvial facies grade basinward into upper delta plain; fan delta facies grade basinward into shelf/platform or into slope clinoforms	Commonly grades shelfward into mounded turbidites or slope clinoforms; may grade laterally into deep-water mounds or fills
Nature of upper/lower boundaries	Concordant, coastal onlap and/or baselap over upper surface; upper surface may be eroded by submarine canyons; basal surface concordant, low-angle baselap or (rare) toplapped by subjacent clinoforms	Normally concordant at top but may be rarely onlapped or baselapped; upper surface may be eroded by submarine canyons; basal surface generally toplapped by prodelta/slope clinoforms (on shelf); rarely concordant with prodelta on shelf but common in deep-water, roll-over anticlines	Upper surface may be onlapped by coastal facies; top may be angular unconformity; base is generally concordant; fan deltas rarely overlie clinoforms (toplap)	Generally concordant at top and base; may onlap eroded slope clinoforms or eroded mounds; upper surface rarely eroded
Amplitude	High	High in delta front and coal/ lignite or marine transgressive facies within delta plain; low/ moderate in most delta plain and in prodelta where in continuity with delta front	Variable—low/high	Low to moderate
Continuity	High	High in delta front, coal/ lignite and marine transgressive facies; low/moderate in remainder of delta plain and prodelta where in lateral continuity with delta front	Discontinuous; continuity decreases landward	High
Frequency (cycle breadth)	Broad or moderate; little variability	Variable; broader in delta front; coal/lignite and marine transgressive facies moderate; narrower in other delta plain and prodelta where in continuity with delta front	Variable; generally narrower cycles than shelf/platform	Generally narrower than shelf/platform; commonly very uniform breadth throughout

*Modified from Vail et al. (1977, pp. 166-168); changes by Brown and Fisher.

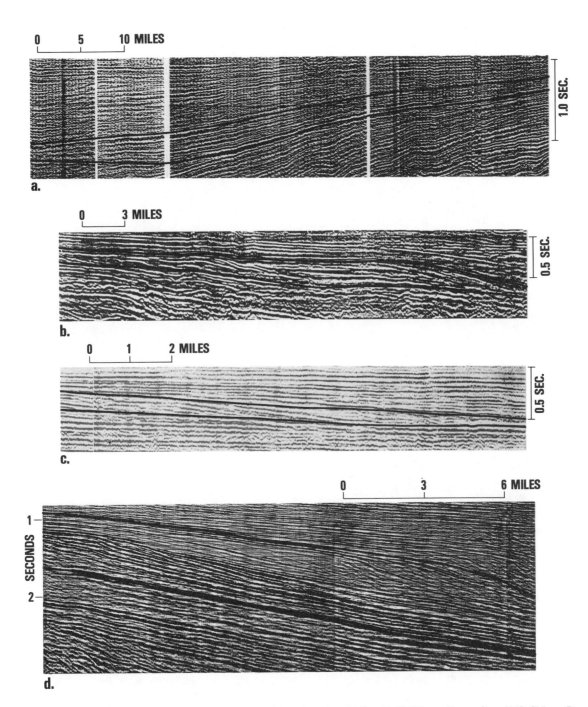

Figure 23. Sigmoid, oblique, and complex sigmoid-oblique reflection configurations.(A) Sigmoid. (B) Oblique with some Sigmoid. (C) Oblique. (D) Complex Sigmoid-oblique. From Mitchum et al. (1977).

Oblique configurations are distinguished by toplap termination of clinoform reflections (fig. 24B). Inclined reflections terminate abruptly updip against the base of parallel/divergent reflections of either shelf/platform or delta platform (undaform, Rich, 1952). Basal downlap (or baselap) terminations may vary from high-angle to tangential. *Sigmoid* configurations, on the other hand, lack toplap terminations and the reflections may be traced updip into parallel/divergent undaform reflections (fig. 24A).

Reflection configurations differ on dip and strike sections. On strike sections (parallel to associated shelf edge) progradational seismic facies exhibit subparallel, generally hummocky to mounded configurations. Clinoform and mounded configurations occur because of the fan-shaped geometry of the facies (and slope system). With a point-source sediment supply along the shelf edge, submarine fan/slope deposits resemble bisected cones in three-dimensional geometry. Consequently, stratal surfaces and resulting seismic reflections within this seismic facies exhibit the typical clinoform in dip-orientation and oriented mounds in strike sections.

Lateral relationships are generally predictive in progradational seismic facies. Clinoform reflections (fig. 23) either extend updip across facies boundaries into undaform configurations (sigmoid type) or terminate (toplap) updip at the base of similar undaform reflections (oblique type). Downdip, progradational facies generally grade into basinal plain or drape facies (e.g., fig. 3). Along strike progradational slope facies exhibit subparallel, continuous to disrupted, hummocky clinoforms and mound configurations. On shallow shelf areas, thin oblique prodelta/slope configurations may grade basinward over a subjacent shelf edge into divergent configurations associated with growth faults and roll-over anticlines of deep-water (shelf-margin) delta origin. Oblique and sigmoid slope configurations may be intergradational.

Boundary relationships are also predictable. By definition progradational seismic facies baselap over subjacent facies. Prodelta/ slope clinoforms on a shelf (fig. 19) generally baselap over shelf or platform facies, but in deep water environments large prodelta/slope clinoforms baselap onto basinal plain or continental rise (onlapping) facies. Deep-water deltaic deposition is normally complicated by growth faults, shale ridges, and roll-over anticlines (fig. 17). Slope clinoforms associated with shelf/platform progradation rarely exhibit growth faults and generally baselap tangentially on basinal plain, continental rise onlap, or mounded/draped seismic facies.

A series of progradational reflections that are internally concordant reflect steady progradation. We have observed minor onlap sequences within major oblique progradational seismic facies (Brown and Fisher, 1977). These minor onlap sequences terminate updip against locally eroded clinoforms; the erosional surfaces are generally part of localized slope and submarine canyon erosional episodes (see later discussions). The youngest (basinward) clinoforms to be deposited in sigmoid, oblique, or any other progradational seismic facies are typically onlapped by deep-water facies (marine onlap, Vail et al., 1977; continental rise onlap, Brown and Fisher, 1977). Extensive submarine erosion characterizes the youngest (basinward) slope clinoforms in most basins (see Woodbine system, fig. 19) and slope in front of Upper Jurassic shelf/platform (fig. 9). We have observed that slope clinoforms deposited during shelf/platform progradation are almost always eroded and onlapped by deep-water facies when slope progradation terminated.

As noted, progradational seismic facies exhibit diagnostic and predictable reflection configurations, geometries, and lateral/bounding relationships. Wave-form parameters are less diagnostic, but some generalizations are possible. Continuity is generally highest in sigmoid facies and lowest in oblique facies. Similarly, amplitudes are commonly high in sigmoid types and lower in oblique reflections, especially along the mid and lower parts of oblique clinoforms. Cycles are generally broader in upper and mid clinoforms of sigmoid facies (thicker beds) and narrow gradually basinward. Cycles are generally narrower on oblique clinoforms and also narrow basinward. Oblique cycles, however, are commonly less uniform and more erratic along the clinoforms. Sigmoid reflections exhibit exceptional continuity and uniformity of amplitude/cycle breadth along strike profiles; oblique reflections are considerably more erratic and discontinuous.

What do different types of progradational reflections mean? Vail et al. (1977) relate sigmoid and oblique clinoforms to "energy" levels (fig. 25). They note that oblique progradation is commonly associated with delta systems and sigmoid seismic facies are commonly deposited during progradation of a shelf or platform edge. Hence, they infer that oblique facies result from high energy deltaic deposition and sigmoid facies from low energy deposition. Vail et al. (1977) suggest that high energy systems will be sand-prone.

CONTROL OF OFFLAP STYLE

° Oblique: rapid deposition relative to
   subsidence or relative rise of sea level
° Sigmoid: slow deposition relative to
   subsidence or relative rise of sea level
° Slope of clinoform controlled by water
   depth and composition of slope sediment

We have made similar observations, but we judge the cause of oblique and sigmoid reflections is more complicated than differences in depositional energy. We have observed that oblique progradation is generally associated either with deltaic progradation or with neritic shelf/platform environments that are repeatedly prograded by updip deltas or fan-deltas. Consequently, oblique clinoforms are commonly composed of terrigenous clastics and these clinoforms *generally* indicate higher sand content updip (on the shelf) in shallow-marine delta or fan-delta facies. Although we concur with Vail et al. (1977) that sigmoids generally are associated with progradation of shelf/platform systems, depositional energy may be either high (reef limestone) or low (micritic limestone). Consequently, we prefer to relate offlap style to rates of deposition relative to subsidence or sea level rise rather than to relative depositional energy. For example, under the same rate of sea level rise and/or basin subsidence a delta system or a shelf-edge, which is periodically supplied by a delta or fan-delta, simply will prograde (shift basinward) more rapidly (oblique)

47

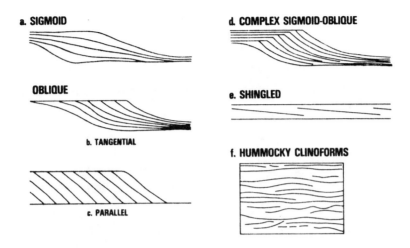

Figure 24. Progradational seismic reflection patterns. From Mit chum et al. (1977).

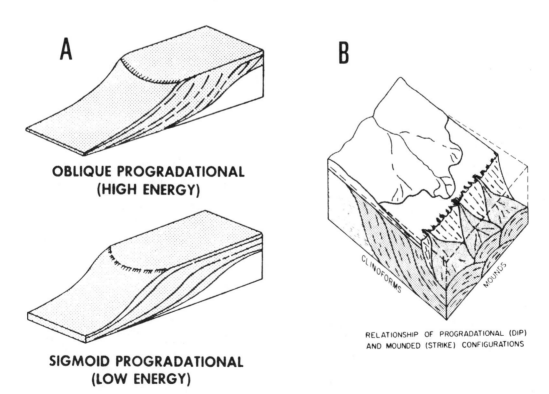

Figure 25. A. Shelf-margin and progradational slope seismic facies. From Sangree and Widmier (1977). B. Relationship between progradational and mounded seismic facies.

than a shelf/platform supplied only with indigenous biogenic sediment originating in shelf-edge environments (sigmoid). Wave and current energy may be the same at a shelf-edge reef or at a shelf-margin delta; it is the capacity for more rapid sedimentation by the delta which causes oblique slope sedimentation. In Brazilian basins during passive-margin conditions (Late Cretaceous) oblique progradation occurred basinward of carbonate shelf margins supplied periodically by fan-deltas. An abrupt shift occurred (mid-Tertiary) to sigmoid progradation and extensive carbonate platform aggradation when the terrigenous clastic supply diminished. Style of offlap may be dictated by volume of sediment introduced to the slope and the rate of sea level rise and/or basin subsidence. The slope or gradient of the clinoform reflection (and slope facies) generally steepens into progressively deeper water. Also, we have observed that calcareous hemipelagic slope deposits appear to support steeper depositional slopes than fine-grained terrigenous clastic facies.

In our judgment it is possible to infer the composition of progradational seismic facies with considerable reliability, in addition to interpreting sediment source and principal depositional processes. When integrated with other seismic facies, the progradational style allows the interpreter to make some reliable predictions about the entire depositional sequence and its internal facies composition. The following table modified from Vail et al. (1977, pp. 166-168) summarizes key factors involved in interpretation of progradational seismic configurations (table 2).

Mounded/Draped Configurations

These reflection configurations occur in response to facies deposited within two distinctive geologic settings--deep-water clastic slope/basin environments and carbonate shelf/platform environments. Clastic mounds on shelf that can be resolved by conventional seismic methods are normally thick delta systems which can be observed best on strike profiles (fig. 18). Obviously a first-order criterion to interpret mounded configurations is discrimination between shelf/platform areas and deep-water parts of a basin.

Table 2. Summary of seismic facies characterized by progradational reflection configurations*

Properties of Seismic Facies	Depositional Environments/Settings	
	Slope: *associated with prograding shelf/platform*	Prodelta/Slope: *associated with prograding shelf delta or shelf-margin delta; or* Slope: *associated with prograding neritic shelf supplied periodically by shelf delta/fan delta*
Reflection configuration	Sigmoid clinoforms Progradational in dip profile; parallel to disrupted and mounded in strike profile	Oblique clinoforms Progradational in dip profile; hummocky, progradational to mounded in strike profile; mounds more common in deep-water slope than in prodelta/slope on shelf
Lithofacies and composition	Hemipelagic slope facies in upper/mid-clinoform; submarine fans common in lower clinoform; generally calcareous clay, silt and some sand (base of clinoform); clinoform deposited in deep water beyond shelf edge	*On shelf:* prodelta (upper) and shallow slope facies (mid-clinoform and lower clinoform); deposited on submerged shelf; composition generally terrigenous clay, silt and sand; sand concentrated in submarine fans at base of clinoform *Beyond shelf edge:* (1) prodelta and deep-water slope associated with shelf-margin delta; may be growth-faulted; clay, silt and sand (in basal submarine fans); and (2) deep-water slope associated with prograding neritic shelf supplied periodically by shelf deltas/fan deltas; clay, silt and sand (in basal submarine fans)
Geometry and structure	Lens-shaped slope system; poorly defined individual submarine fans and point sources; strike profile may intersect facies to define parallel to slightly mounded configurations; rarely affected by growth faults; represents low rate of sedimentation under relatively uniform sea level rise and/or subsidence rate	Complex fan geometry with apices at shelf-edge point sources; each submarine fan resembles a bisected cone; total slope system lens- to wedge-shaped; strike profiles intersect fans or cones to display complex mounds; seismic facies deposited rapidly relative to subsidence and/or sea level rise; highly unstable slopes associated with deep-water deltas (growth faults, roll-over anticlines)
Lateral relationships	Grades updip through shelf/platform edge facies into parallel/divergent shelf/platform (undaform) reflections; may grade downdip into basinal plain (fondoform) or mound/drape seismic facies; grades along strike to similar facies; may change landward to oblique facies	Terminates updip against base of delta platform or shelf/platform (undaform) facies and may grade downdip into basinal plain (fondoform), or mound/drape facies; may change basinward into sigmoid facies; grade along strike into mounded facies and locally submarine canyon-fill facies
Nature of upper/lower boundaries	Generally concordant at top and downlap (baselap) terminations at base; upper surface of outer or distal sigmoids may be eroded by submarine erosion and submarine canyons; eroded surface commonly onlapped by continental rise facies	Toplap termination at top and downlap (baselap) termination at base; may contain local or minor submarine erosion/onlap sequences; outer or distal oblique clinoforms commonly eroded by submarine erosion and submarine canyon cutting; eroded surface generally onlapped by continental rise facies
Amplitude	Moderate to high; uniform	Moderate to high in upper clinoform; moderate to low in lower clinoform; highly variable
Continuity	Generally continuous	Generally continuous in upper clinoform; discontinuous in mid-clinoform and lower clinoform; may exhibit better continuity near base
Frequency (cycle breadth)	Broadest in mid-clinoform where beds thickest; uniform along strike	Broadest at top and generally decreases downdip as beds thin; variable along strike

*Modified from Vail et al. (1977, pp. 166-168); changes by Brown and Fisher.

SEISMIC FACIES TYPES

Mounded and draped configurations
° Shelf carbonates/mounds/drapes
° Delta (strike sections) mounds
° Deepwater: turbidites (mounds)
  and hemipelagics (drapes)

Shelf mounded configurations generally coincide with biogenic carbonate buildups such as shelf-edge, reef, or bank. Superposed strata may drape over mounds. Slope/basin mounded configurations are in response to thick submarine fans deposited at the foot of a slope. Such fans generally are composed of proximal turbidites and commonly reflect significant mass gravity transport (slumping). Deep-water mounds may fill low areas to produce complex mounded to chaotic-fill facies. We will consider carbonate and clastic mounds independently since they represent entirely different depositional processes and require different recognition criteria.

Modern studies of *carbonate facies* permit conventional stratigraphers to distinguish and to map a great variety of facies that compose carbonate shelf/platform systems (fig. 26). Resolution of current seismic methods, however, permits recognition only of thicker, more distinctive carbonate facies or associations of facies. Such elements include elongate shelf/platform margins, local patch and pinnacle reefs, and elongate barrier reefs (fig. 27). Equivalent back-shelf, fore-reef, and basinal carbonate facies also can be inferred when a shelf edge has been recognized. Bubb and Hatlelid (in Vail et al., 1977) proposed three kinds of criteria for recognizing carbonate buildups: (1) direct criteria including reflections that outline buildups and lateral changes in reflection properties that indicate a facies change; (2) indirect criteria including drape of superposed strata over buildups, velocity pull-ups (or pull-downs), and diffraction/sideswipe along margins of buildups; and (3) basin architecture which permits use of structural elements (i.e., hinge lines, fault-blocks) as guides to preferred carbonate depositional settings. Onlap of slope reflections against

51

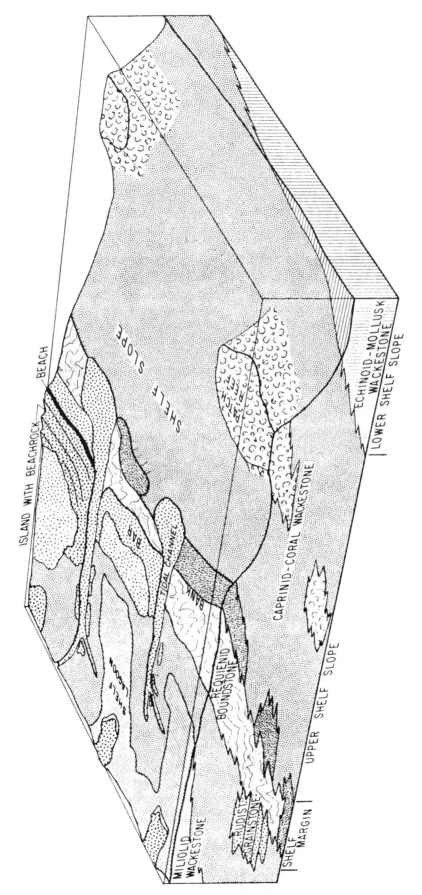

Figure 26. Facies and interpreted depositional environments across the Stuart City Trend, South Texas. From Bebout (1974).

52

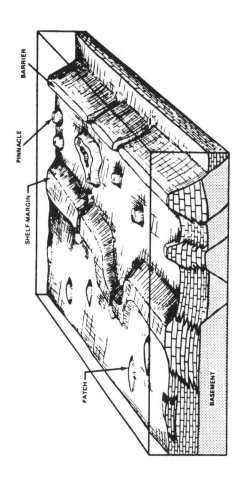

Figure 27. Types of carbonate buildups most easily recognized on seismic profiles. From Bubb and Hatlelid (1977).

abandoned and eroded shelf/platform edges (figs. 9, 19, 29) is a very typical characteristic of carbonate systems.

Direct evidence of the boundary of a carbonate buildup generally relies upon reflections directly from the surface of the buildup and, if depositional relief was sufficient, flanking onlap reflections against the buildup (figs. 9, 19, 28, 29). Lateral changes in wave properties (amplitude, continuity, frequency) are also common. For example, high amplitude/continuity reflections from well bedded back-reef shelf strata generally grade basinward into chaotic or reflector-free reef or shelf-edge bank facies, and, in turn, basinward (downdip) into proximal, steeply inclined chaotic facies reflections, and distally into deep-water limestone facies characterized by high amplitude, continuity, and narrower cycle breadth (figs. 19, 29). These dip-oriented seismic facies changes are diagnostic of carbonate shelf/platform and basinal depositional systems throughout the world (fig. 14) and permit some prediction of lateral changes in lithofacies properties (i.e., bedding, velocity, porosity/density, fluid content).

Indirect evidence generally involves drape of strata over carbonate buildups, evidence of velocity pull-ups, and spurious events such as diffractions/sideswipe because of abrupt lateral velocity changes (fig. 30). Very subtle indirect effects are velocity pull-up and drape, as well as evidence of flexuring and bed thinning (fig. 31).

Configuration of reflections provides the best guide to interpret carbonate seismic facies. Shelf-edge buildups are commonly reflector-free or chaotic and they generally grade landward into shelf/platform reflections and basinward into progradational (generally sigmoid) clino-forms (fig. 29) and ultimately into basinal plain hemipelagic facies. Shelf reflections commonly diverge into a shelf or platform-edge bank or reef buildup (fig. 31). Carbonate pinnacles and barriers exhibit similar relationships with flanking reflections.

External geometry of shelf/platform-edge or barrier carbonate seismic facies is generally an elongate lens parallel to the relict shelf edge. Back-shelf patch and pinnacle reefs may be subcircular to elongate lenses parallel to shelf edge. Carbonate buildups are normally concordant at the base and top. Buildup may overlie sigmoid (and rarely

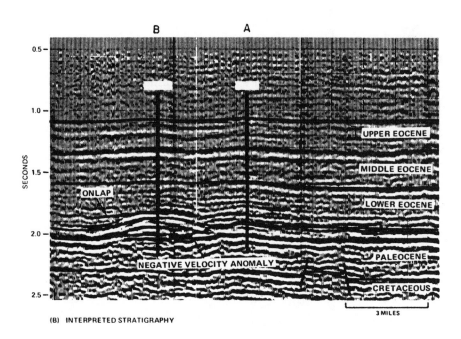

Figure 28. Pinnacle reef, Tertiary North Africa. Shows buildups, onlap cycles, overlying drape, and negative velocity anomaly. 12-fold CDP thumper data. From Bubb and Hatlelid (1977).

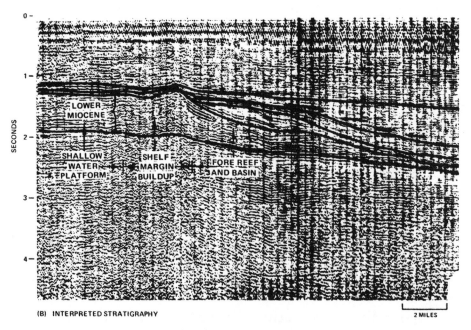

Figure 29. Miocene back-shelf, shelf-margin reef, and marine (slope) onlap, Gulf of Papua. 6-fold CDP dynamite data. From Bubb and Hatlelid (1977).

55

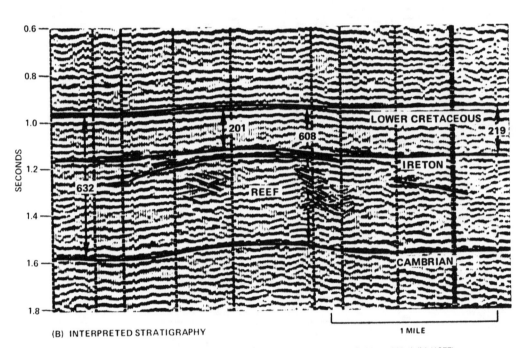

(B) INTERPRETED STRATIGRAPHY

1 MILE

Figure 30. Devonian reef buildup, Yekau Lake, Alberta. From Bubb and Hatlelid (1977).

56

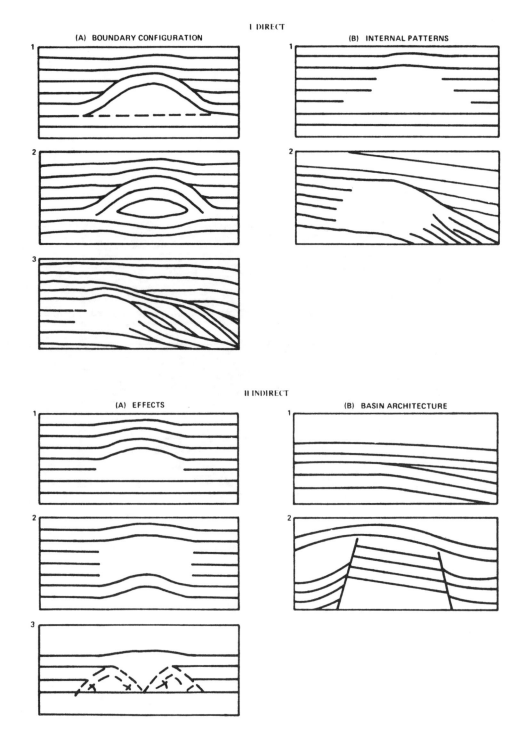

Figure 31. Criteria for recognizing carbonate buildups on seismic profiles. From Bubb and Hatlelid (1977).

oblique) clinoforms (fig. 14). Concordant drape (figs. 19, 29) generally characterizes upper boundaries.

Bubb and Hatlelid (in Vail et al., 1977) summarized types of evidence for recognizing carbonate buildups (fig. 31). Geologists ex-
perienced in carbonate facies can infer specific facies and potential
reservoir properties once the facies have been delineated and mapped.

Clastic mounded and/or draped seismic facies that can be resolved
by conventional reflection seismic methods are deposited in environments
basinward of shelf edges (fig. 32). Mounds are constructed by slumping
and dense turbidity flow (or other types of grain flow) down along
basinal or continental slopes. Deposition of mounded submarine fans
generally occurs at the distal end of a submarine canyon system. Mound
composition depends upon the composition of shelf and slope sediment
that served as a source. Mounds are normally composed of sand and shale
with thin, intercalated calcareous clays. Mound deposition commonly
coincides with periods of canyon erosion and onlap against eroded slopes
or in bathymetric lows in front of slopes (see Heritier et al., 1979).

Draped configurations, if present, result from long periods of hemipelagic sedimentation (from suspension) which blankets the basinal plain
and bathymetric relief. Drape sheets mirror the paleobathymetric surface. It is common to observe drapes overlying mounds that were eroded
by submarine currents probably associated with emplacement of the
turbidites (fig. 33). Even mounds not covered by drape sheets commonly
exhibit eroded upper surfaces (fig. 32). Draped facies may be terrigenous or calcareous clay-sized sediment and pelagic oozes. Cycles of
terrigenous/calcareous hemipelagic sediment occur in response to
periodic slumping and turbidity flow down nearby slopes (terrigenous
sedimentation) followed by longer periods of suspension deposition of
calcareous oozes. Impedance differences between terrigenous and calcareous sheets are probably responsible for the well layered character
displayed on high resolution seismic lines and for relatively continuous,
moderate amplitude reflections with narrow cycle breadth that characterize
drapes shown on conventional seismic records.

We noted that progradational seismic facies, especially oblique,
exhibit mounded character in strike profiles. Catastrophic erosion and

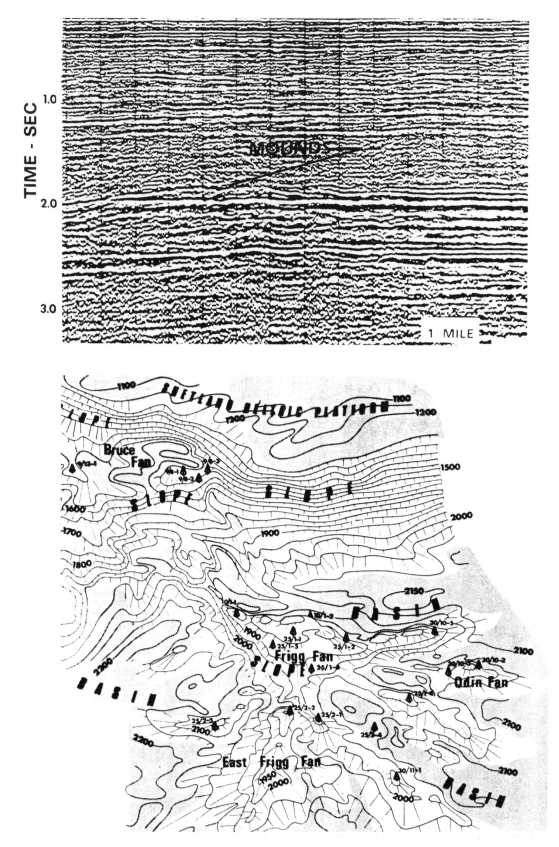

Figure 32. Deep-water, mounded seismic facies, submarine fan complex, North Sea Basin. A. Seismic profile of Frigg Fan. From Sangree and Widmier (1977). B. Paleogeography and inferred paleobathymetry of Frigg and associate fans. From Heritier et al. (1979).

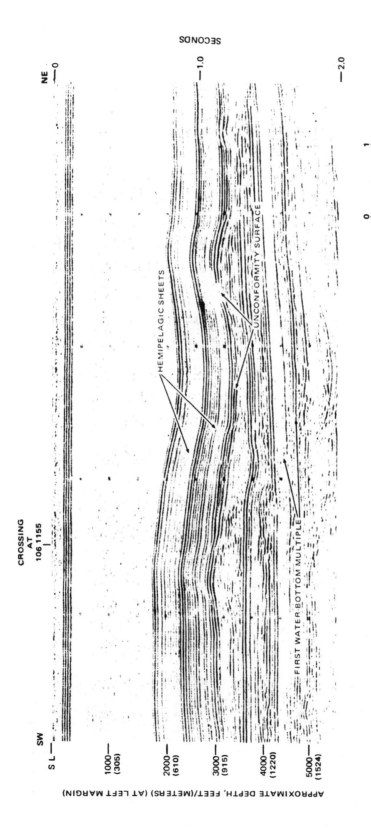

Figure 33. Draped deep-water seismic facies over mounded seismic facies, Pleistocene, Gulf of Mexico. From Sangree and Widmier (1977).

slumping probably account for most deep-water mounds composed of poorly sorted to chaotic sediments. If the sediment supply is coarse-grained and/or if blocks of shelf-edge and upper slope sediment compose the mounds, differential compaction generally exaggerates the bathymetric relief on the mound surface. As mentioned, alternating turbidity and hemipelagic deposition produce thick mounds of sand and shale (with chaotic or poorly layered reflections) with thin, intercalated calcareous hemipelagic draped layers (high amplitude/continuity). Figure 34 illustrates a sandy, deep-water mound that gradually onlapped the floor of a major depression (the fault was post-depositional); high amplitude/ continuity reflections are probably in response to thin, calcareous hemipelagic drapes intercalated with thicker sandy turbidite deposits.

Clastic mounds are characterized by poorly organized layered or chaotic reflections (fig. 35) of poor continuity, generally low amplitude, and variable cycle breadth. Intercalated hemipelagic facies and well developed draped facies exhibit moderate amplitude, high continuity reflections with uniform but narrow cycle breadth.

Mounds may be fan-shaped, subcircular, or irregular in plan view and may vary from biconvex (in onlap fill settings, fig. 34) to more typical plano-convex (upward) (figs. 32, 33). Draped configurations are sheet-like blankets of hemipelagic sediment (fig. 33). Mounds may grade updip into other mounds, onlap canyon-fill facies, or, rarely, onlap progradational clinoforms. Downdip, mounds grade into basinal plain (fondoform) or drape seismic facies. Along strike, mounds and drapes commonly are intergradational. Draped seismic facies normally grade shelfward into mounded facies, into fill facies or into progradational facies. Draped facies may grade any direction into basinal plain (fondoform) facies; drapes thin away from shelf/slope sediment sources.

The base of mounds is normally concordant, although onlap mounds exhibit basal onlap (figs. 32, 33). Complex mounds may display baselap and even hummocky clinoforms. The upper surface of mounds may be concordant, but more commonly it is erosional and overlain by draped configurations or baselapping progradational clinoforms (fig. 33). Draped seismic facies are normally concordant at base and top but they may exhibit subtle onlap. Drapes commonly overlie eroded mounds. Drapes

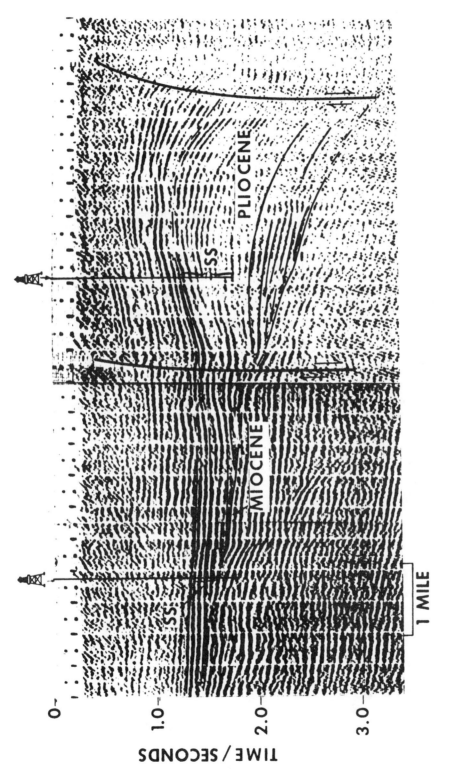

Figure 34. Mounded onlap-fill seismic facies, Pliocene, offshore California. From Sangree and Widmier (1977).

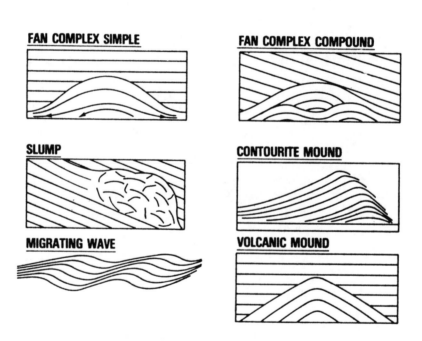

Figure 35. Clastic mounded seismic facies configurations. From Mitchum et al. (1977).

may be overlain by mounds, by baselapping clinoforms, or rarely by onlapping fills.

We have noted that mounded seismic configurations may occur within bathymetric depressions and submarine canyons where they normally are classified as onlap-fill facies. Fill and mounded seismic facies are characteristic of deep-water environments and constitute an intergradational class of turbidite seismic facies. Another type of mounded seismic facies exhibited along the seaward margin of the Blake Plateau, southeastern U. S. continental margin (Shipley et al., 1978),has been attributed to geostrophic or contour currents (fig. 35). We have not observed this seismic facies elsewhere.

In summary, we have found that mounded seismic facies can be interpreted with a reasonable degree of accuracy, especially when the interpreter has been able to define relict shelf edges within the basin. Direct and indirect criteria enable one to recognize carbonate mounded facies (fig. 31). Deep-water mounds normally (fig. 35) are clastic in composition and indicate a variety of turbidity and slump processes that redeposit outer shelf/upper slope sediments on the nearby basin floor. Thick draped facies indicate periods of hemipelagic suspension deposition. Both carbonate and clastic mounds may serve as significant petroleum reservoirs. The table modified from Vail et al. (1977, pp. 166-168) summarizes criteria useful in interpreting mounded/draped seismic facies (table 3).

Onlap and Fill Configurations

Onlap and fill configurations are among the most common reflection terminations in a basin. Onlap terminations may occur in response to shallow coastal (paralic) facies deposited when sea level rise and/or basin subsidence shifted the nearshore coastal environments progressively landward. We will see later that transgression of the actual coast line may not necessarily coincide with *coastal onlap* (Vail et al., 1977). Locally, subtle onlap of shelf and platform facies also may occur against the flanks of reefs, banks or against the flanks of shallow shelf depressions.

A second common class of onlap reflections occur in response to deep-water facies deposited beyond a shelf-edge. This has been called

Table 3. Summary of seismic facies
characterized by mounded and draped reflection configuration*

Properties of Seismic Facies	Depositional Environments/Settings		
	Reefs and Banks: *shelf/platform margin, back shelf patch reefs and pinnacle/barrier reefs*	Submarine Canyon and Lower Slope: *proximal turbidities, slumped clastics*	Hemipelagic Clastics: *proximal basin and lower slope*
Reflection configuration	Mounded, chaotic, or reflector-free; pull-up or pull-down common	Mounded; complex and variable	Parallel; mirrors underlying surface
Lithofacies and composition	Shallow-water carbonate biogenic buildups; may or may not exhibit reef-forming framework	Sand and shale submarine fans; complex gravity-failure fans or mounds; turbidity flow; other grain flows, submarine landslides/debris flows; clinoform/ fondoform deposits	Terrigenous and calcareous clays (commonly alternating); pelagic oozes; deposition from suspension plumes and nepheloid clouds; fondoform deposits
Geometry and structure	Elongate lens-shaped (shelf/ platform edge and barrier reefs); elongate to subcircular lens-shaped (patch and pinnacle reefs/banks); form on stable structural elements	Irregular fan-shaped to mounded geometry; common but not restricted to unstable basins	Sheet to blanket geometry exhibiting drape over underlying surface; common in deep, subsiding basins
Lateral relationships	Shelf/platform edge facies grade updip into parallel/ divergent shelf/platform facies; grade downdip into talus and sigmoid clinoform facies; patch reef/bank facies grade updip and downdip into parallel/divergent shelf/ platform facies; pinnacle and barrier facies grade downdip into talus clino- forms and to basinal plain (fondoform) facies	May grade shelfward into progradational clinoforms (normally oblique), canyon onlap fill, or pinch out against eroded slope; may grade basinward and laterally into basinal plain (fondoform); onlap fills or drapes	Commonly grades laterally or basinward into basinal plain (fondoform) facies; may grade shelfward into submarine canyon onlap fill; may onlap eroded slope
Nature of upper and lower boundaries	Upper surface concordant or may be onlapped by flank reflections; basal surface concordant, base- lapping, or may overlie clinoform toplap; pull-up or pull-down of basal surface common	Upper surface commonly erosional and onlapped, baselapped, or concordant (with drape); basal surface irregularly baselapping; may appear concordant (low resolution), or may onlap (mounded onlap fill)	Upper surface commonly concordant, but may be onlapped or baselapped; basal surface generally concordant but may onlap eroded mound or slope
Amplitude	High along boundaries; may be moderate to low internally; commonly reflector-free	Variable; generally low; some higher internal amplitudes may be thin hemipelagic drapes	Low to moderate; some high amplitude reflections (well defined on high-frequency, shallow data)
Continuity	High along boundaries; internally discontinuous to reflector-free	Discontinuous to chaotic	High
Frequency (cycle breadth)	Broad; cycle may diverge into massively bedded buildup	Highly variable; commonly narrow	Narrow, uniform

*Modified from Vail et al. (1977, pp. 166-168); changes by Brown and Fisher.

marine onlap (Vail et al., 1977). It includes a variety of seismic
facies, most of which also display some degree of *onlap fill*, characterized by reflection terminations against the sides of basin-floor depressions, against the walls of eroded canyons and troughs, and landward against eroded slope clinoforms. Thick, widespread deep-water
(marine) onlap facies, which probably represent coalescence of many
deep-water fan and hemipelagic deposits, have been called continental
rises by oceanographers. These submarine physiographic and stratigraphic elements are common on modern and ancient passive continental
margins. We have applied the term *continental rise onlap* to widespread
seismic facies analogous to modern rises. *Slope front onlap fills*
(Vail et al., 1977) are generally analogous except that rise seismic
facies may exhibit a much more subtle base lap (basinward) onto basinal
plain or draped facies. Other more restricted deep-water onlap reflections have been named by Vail et al. (1977) according to respective
internal configurations: chaotic, mounded, prograded, and divergent.
We also separately distinguish onlap fill within submarine canyons.

SEISMIC FACIES TYPES

Onlap/fill configurations
° Coastal (paralic) onlap
° Continental rise (slope
  front) onlap
° Canyon onlap fill
° Chaotic, mounded, prograded
  divergent onlap fills

Deep water
(marine)
onlaps

Vail et al. (1977) do not designate *coastal onlap* reflections as
seismic facies. Rather, they are primarily concerned with the relative
sea level significance of coastal onlap (fig. 36). These landward terminating reflections are evidence of the landward limits of paralic sedimentation. Paleontologic identification of shallow marine facies would
be ideal to mark an actual sea level position but such data are rare.
Landward termination of coastal onlap reflections in most basins actually

represents the onlap of low gradient, subaerial alluvial deposits onto the eroded coastal plain. Because of low gradients, termination actually may be a few meters above mean sea level as Vail et al. (1977) indicated, but the terminations approximate sea level.

We use coastal onlap to define proximal delta, fan delta, and shallow shelf/platform seismic facies. Seaward, the boundaries of coastal onlap seismic facies are transitional but in most cases we have been able to recognize a basinward change from alluvial facies to shallow marine. Coastal onlap facies are commonly alluvial or delta plain but shallow marine/supratidal carbonates also may onlap eroded coastal strata. Coastal onlap does not necessarily imply strandline transgression but may coincide with regression or with a stable shoreline position, depending upon the balance between sea level rise, subsidence and sedimentation rates (Vail et al., 1977). Reflection configuration of onlapping coastal deposits are generally parallel/divergent types and the reader is referred to previous discussions and table for description of reflection configurations, geometry, lithofacies composition and amplitude, continuity and frequency of these reflections. Coastal onlap against eroded sea cliffs or high relief shorelines would result in beaches directly over the onlap unconformity but this physiographic setting is rare in a basin supplied with a significant input of fluvial/deltaic sediments. Coastal seismic facies, therefore, represent landward pinchout of nearshore subaerial facies against eroded coastal plain deposits.

Coastal onlap facies may exhibit concordant upper surfaces under continued relative sea level rise. More commonly coastal facies are tilted and eroded, followed by onlap of coastal facies in subsequent sequences. Of course, the base of coastal onlap facies is characterized by onlap termination. Coastal onlap in West Africa (fig. 36) continued from Late Jurassic through Late Cretaceous. This major coastal onlap episode is common along many segments of the Atlantic continental margins following rifting. Post-rift passive-margin subsidence and relative sea level rise combined to produce similar sequences.

Continental rise onlap is also a common seismic facies especially along passive continental margins of the world (fig. 37). Seismic dip pro-

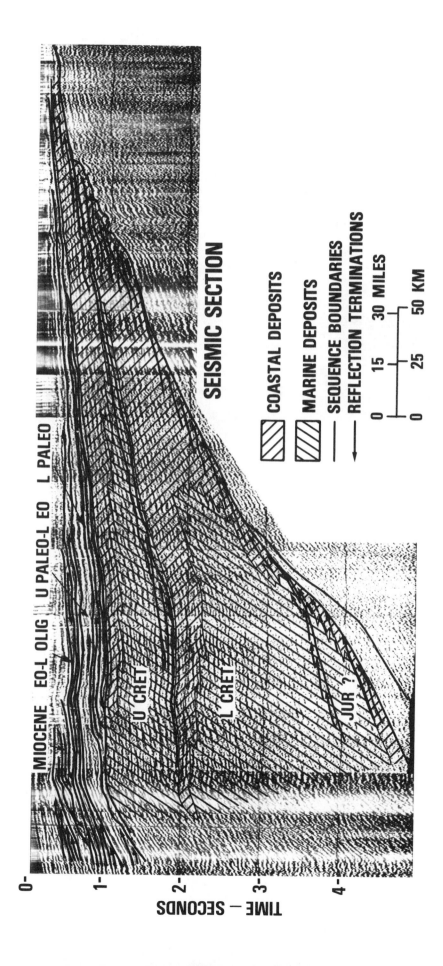

Figure 36. Coastal onlap, offshore West Africa. From Vail et al. (1977).

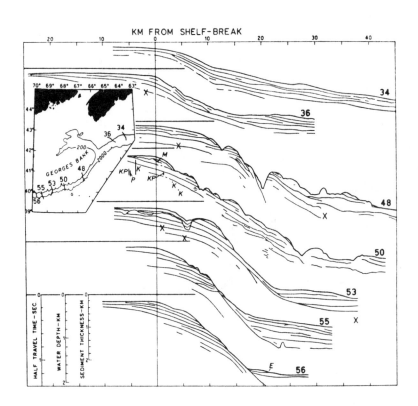

Figure 37. Erosional shelf edges and marine (continental rise) onlap, offshore Nova Scotia and Georges Bank. From Uchupi and Emery (1967).

files (e.g. U.S.G.S. Line 2) in the Baltimore Canyon area of the U. S. Atlantic continental margin clearly show the presence of thick continental rise seismic facies that onlapped eroded Jurassic and Cretaceous strata. Similar thick onlap facies exist in the Gulf of Mexico/Caribbean Basin (fig. 38). Because of salt mobilization, these latter onlap units also exhibit onlap-fill geometry.

Continental rise onlap and slope-front onlap fills most commonly occur basinward of eroded carbonate shelf/platform systems (figs. 19, 29, 39). Marine onlap reflections terminate shelfward into submarine canyon fills, against eroded slope clinoforms, and in some cases, directly onto shelf/platform deposits.

Continental rise and slope-front fill consist of parallel to subparallel reflection configurations. In many cases these facies are shelfward or proximal parts of basinal plain facies. Rise facies are generally fine-grained turbidites and intercalated hemipelagic calcareous clays and pelagic oozes. The seismic facies is lenticular to wedge-shaped, and in plan view may define large submarine fans with apecies extending into the mouths of large submarine canyons. More commonly, continental rise facies were supplied with turbidity and hemipelagic sediment through a myriad of small submarine canyons and gulleys situated along tens or hundreds of kilometers of shelf edges.

Continental rise facies grade basinward into basinal plain or draped facies. Shelfward they terminate abruptly against eroded slope or shelf. Onlap facies are rarely represented by contemporaneous shelf or shallow marine deposits, indicating that during periods of marine onlap deposition was restricted exclusively to deep-water environments.

The top of continental rise facies is generally baselapped (without erosion) by subsequent progradational slope clinoforms or by mounded turbidite deposits. The surface of an onlap rise normally exhibits an exceedingly smooth bathymetric configuration that dips uniformly in a basinward direction. Two or more superposed onlap sequences may be recognized only by subtle onlap terminations. Base of the facies, of course, may onlap bathymetric highs such as mounds, salt, or fault block structures, and eroded slope clinoforms. The unconformity at the base of continental rise facies represents significant hiatuses in many basins. Continental rise facies may extend for hundreds of kilometers along strike; gentle mounded configurations may occur, but they are rarely so pronounced as those exhibited by prograding (offlap) reflections.

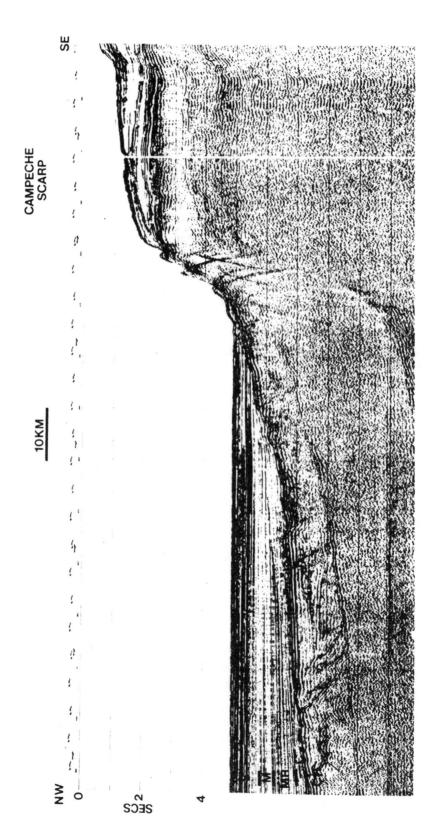

Figure 38. Eroded Campeche scarp and thick marine (continental rise) onlap, Gulf of Mexico basin. From Worzel and Burk (1978).

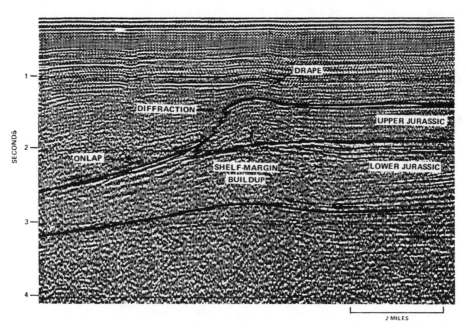

Figure 39. Shelf-margin carbonate buildup, marine onlap and back-shelf seismic facies, offshore West Africa. From Bubb and Hatlelid (1977).

Amplitudes in response to rise facies are generally moderate to low; continuity is generally moderate. Cycle breadth is typically narrow.

Onlap fill reflection configurations exhibit a number of variations depending upon the nature of the trough or depression filled by turbidity currents and submarine gravity slumps. Obviously, less parallel and more chaotic to mounded fill reflections indicate a greater influence of catastrophic deposition. Another variable that affects fill configurations is stability of the depression or trough during deposition. If turbidity deposition fills an existing erosional canyon or trough, reflections generally will be parallel throughout. If the depression subsides during deposition, such as salt withdrawal basin, reflections will be subparallel and generally will converge toward the margin and diverge toward the axis of the active basin. Complex onlap fills also exhibit evidence of multiple source directions including axial and side filling. Consequently, variations in fill configurations provide an interpreter with a variety of ideas concerning sediment source, type of transport processes, and subsidence history, among others.

Submarine canyon onlap fill facies are important elements in reconstructing the depositional history of a basin. Its presence on a seismic profile indicates to the interpreter that the canyon originated up the paleobathymetric slope and extended basinward to a point where paleoslope decreased dramatically, such as the foot of the continental slope. Submarine canyon fill deposits are best recognized in seismic profiles parallel to relict shelf edges and, therefore, normal to paleobathymetric gradient. Profiles that are transverse to canyon systems (fig. 40) exhibit onlap fill with reflections terminating against the erosional unconformity along the channel boundary. On dip profiles, submarine canyon fill reflections onlap landward or up the erosional paleofloor of the canyon.

The basal part of the Mississippi trough or canyon (fig. 40) is filled by mounded onlap deposits and the upper part is clearly an onlap fill sequence. The profile shows parallel deep-water reflections diverging into a salt-withdrawal depression. Some convergence of reflections against the salt structure suggests contemporaneous uplift/deposition. Depth of submarine erosion into a relict clastic sequence can be determined with reasonable accuracy. However, submarine canyons that erode a carbonate shelf or platform may be followed by aggradation (upbuilding) of the carbonate platform facies contemporaneous with canyon-fill deposition. The original canyon depth due to erosion is falsely enhanced by upbuilding of the platform. We have mapped scores of submarine canyon systems in rocks

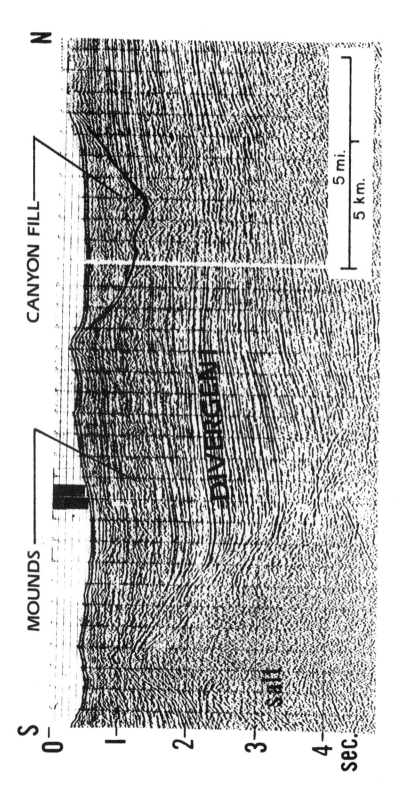

Figure 40. Mississippi Trough, a Pleistocene submarine canyon, Gulf of Mexico. From Stuart and Caughey (1977).

of many ages and have observed submarine erosion as great as 2200 meters. Mapped ancient submarine canyons may be tens of kilometers in length and 20-30 kilometers in width near relict shelf edges. Some canyons bifurcate updip and all canyons disappear landward into uneroded shelf or platform. Broad erosional "reentrants" up to 100 kilometers wide (along strike) may extend tens of kilometers landward into relict shelf systems of passive-margin basins of Brazil. Tongue of the Ocean, a modern submarine canyon extending into the Bahama Platform is up to 4000 meters deep although in part this depth may result from carbonate aggradation on the platform. Such canyons are cut by submarine processes and are not drowned river canyons. There are cases where Pleistocene river valley erosion connects with upper ends of canyons, but the canyons were eroded principally in the submarine environment. Significance of submarine canyons and sea level changes will be discussed later.

Parallel/divergent to mounded or chaotic typify configurations of reflections in submarine canyon-fill facies. Rarely, progradational clinoforms may fill all or part of a canyon. Composition of fills varies from coarse slump and turbidite clastic facies to intercalated hemipelagic facies, and, in shallower updip parts of canyons, neritic shale and limestone facies. Canyons, therefore, are filled with deep-water deposits of a variety of compositions and by a variety of processes. Fill facies generally indicate shallower water depths upward through the sequences. Geometry of canyon-fill facies reflects the elongate shape of the canyons or troughs. Distal parts of canyons may contain submarine fans that onlap up the canyon system. Large reentrants eroded landward into a relict shelf are filled by facies similar to continental rises and slope-front fills. Reentrant-fills are elongate lenses in geometry, reflecting the shape of the broad bathymetric depressions. Channel onlap-fill facies terminate updip and laterally against eroded slope and shelf/platform deposits. Downdip this seismic facies may grade into a variety of submarine fan facies (mounded, chaotic, or parallel) and distally into basinal plain or drape facies.

Top of canyon-fill facies may be concordant with shallow shelf/platform facies in updip areas. We have observed two superposed canyon-fill sequences separated by subtle onlap unconformity. In downdip areas, the fill generally is overlain by downlapped clinoforms. Base of canyon fill, of course, exhibits onlapping terminations landward and along strike against erosional unconformities. Basinward, canyon fill may baselap subtly against mounds, drapes or basinal plain facies. We have observed that the coarsest turbidite deposits occur near the base of the seismic facies.

Amplitudes are variable but generally moderate to low. Continuity is moderate, but intercalated hemipelagic facies may display high continuity. Cycle breadth is generally narrow, but it may broaden toward the axis of the canyon, especially if any subsidence occurred during fill deposition.

Other onlap fill facies reflect deep-water deposition in various basin-floor depressions, both erosional and structural (fig. 41). Structural basins may be fault-bounded, sea-floor grabens or salt withdrawal basins flanked by salt ridges (figs. 42, 43, 44), or rarely, basins flanking shale ridges and diapirs. Low to moderate-density turbidity flow deposits produce parallel/divergent fills (fig. 42). Figure 42 demonstrates long-term onlap fill by low density turbidity flow contemporaneous with basin subsidence. Breadths of cycles are widest in the axes of basins and converge onto the flanks of salt structures. Post-depositional diapiric intrusion would not exhibit divergent patterns and consistent change in cycle breadth.

Catastrophic submarine landslide deposition and dense turbidity flow alternate with periods of slow hemipelagic deposition to produce a fill facies that is common in salt-withdrawal basins (fig. 42) and in basins flanking shale diapiric structures. Petroleum occurs in Late Tertiary coarse-grained turbidity deposits in basins between shale diapiric structures in southeastern Niger delta. Figure 43 illustrates a fill composed of hemipelagic onlap facies, a chaotic submarine slump/turbidity flow onlap facies, followed by more hemipelagic onlap fill facies. Even better illustrated chaotic/mounded onlap fills are shown in figure 43.

The character of onlap fill seismic facies generally resemble their respective non-fill analogues: i.e. parallel/divergent basinal facies, mounded/chaotic facies, and hemipelagic draped facies. Refer to these non-fill analogues for description of seismic and stratigraphic character. Fill geometry and basal onlap terminations set the fill facies apart from other deep-water seismic facies.

Vail et al. (1977) summarized some of the principal deep-water seismic facies deposited on slope and basin floors (fig. 45). These include fill, mounded,and draped configurations. The following table modified from Vail et al. (1977, pp. 166-168) summarizes criteria for interpreting onlap and fill seismic facies (table 4).

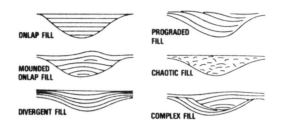

Figure 41. Fill seismic facies configurations. From Mitchum et al. (1977).

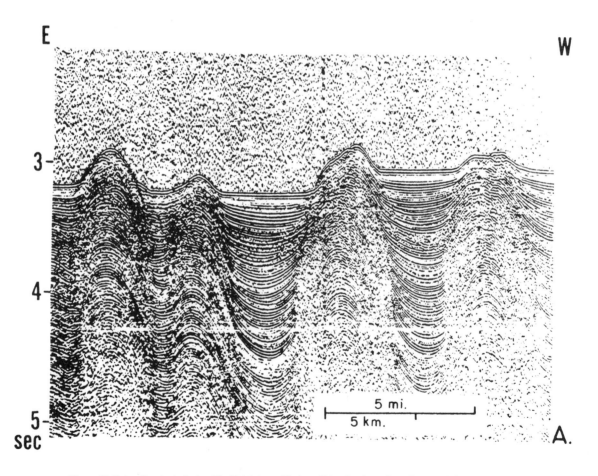

Figure 42. Onlap fill seismic facies, Plio-Pleistocene, Mexican Ridge Province. From Stuart and Caughey (1977).

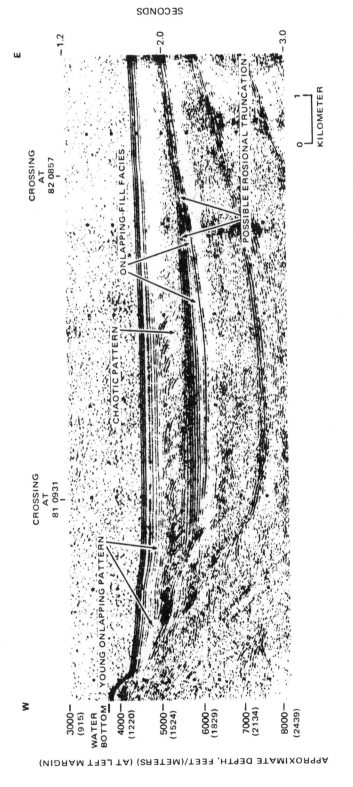

Figure 43. Onlap-fill seismic facies, Pleistocene Gulf of Mexico. Hemipelagic facies enveloping clastic turbidity deposit. From Sangree and Widmier (1977).

UNCONFORMITIES RECOGNIZED BY
REFLECTION TERMINATIONS

Truncated Reflections

° Tilted and truncated reflections: regional
  angular unconformity; generally subaerial
  erosion

° Local truncation of reflections: submarine
  canyons and eroded mounds

Lapout Reflections

° Onlap, downlap, and toplap: non-depositional
  unconformities

Concordant Reflections

° Concordant reflections that can be traced
  laterally into unconformity inferred from
  truncation or lapout

NOTE: Presence of a reflection directly in response
to the unconformity depends upon the velocity/density
contrast across the unconformity: reflection may be
continuous, discontinuous, or missing.

Recognizing and Evaluating Unconformities

Seismic stratigraphic analysis is an excellent means of identifying
and interpreting unconformities (fig. 46). Of course, with sufficient
paleontologic and conventional stratigraphic data from the subsurface,
recognition of unconformities is possible. Nevertheless, many of them,
especially the lapout non-depositional unconformities, realistically can
be recognized and evaluated *only* by seismic-stratigraphic interpretation
(figs. 11, 12). Using simple concepts of a cross cutting (erosion) and
superposition (depositional order), the interpreter can make qualitative
estimates of hiatuses or time gaps represented by an unconformity (fig.
47). Paleontologic zones established from well cuttings can be correlated using isochronous (stratal) reflections to establish age relationships along an unconformity--hence the magnitude of the unconformity can
be determined along its extent. Of course, faults terminate reflections
and the interpreter must distinguish between structural termination and
erosional/deposition terminations.

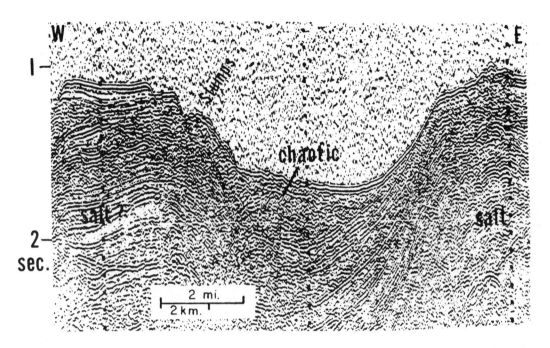

Figure 44. Clastic-fill seismic facies, Pleistocene, western Louisiana slope. From Stuart and Caughey (1977).

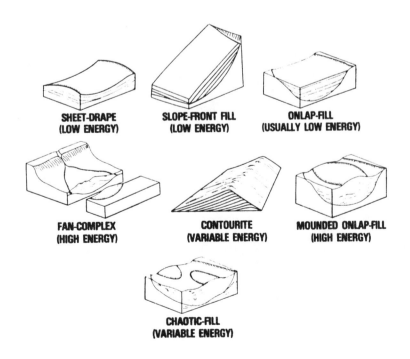

Figure 45. Slope and basin-floor seismic facies configurations and geometry. From Sangree and Widmier (1977).

Table 4. Summary of seismic facies characterized by onlap and fill reflection configurations*

Properties of Seismic Facies	Depositional Environments/Settings			
	Coastal (Paralic) Onlap Facies	Continental Rise: *slope-front fill and onlap clastics*	Submarine Canyon-Fill Deposits	Other Deep-Water Fill Deposits: *mounded, chaotic, structurally active basins*
Reflection configuration	Parallel; coastal onlap	Parallel/divergent; platform or shelfward onlap	Parallel/divergent; landward and lateral onlap	Parallel/divergent; chaotic, mounded onlap
Lithofacies and composition	Delta/alluvial plain and medial fan delta sands and shales; supratidal clastic/carbonate facies; rarely beach/shoreface clastic facies	Sand and shale deposited in submarine fans by turbidity flows; hemipelagic terrigenous/calcareous clays; distal pelagic oozes	Sand and shale deposited by turbidity flow in submarine fans near base; hemipelagic and neritic shale/ calcareous clays in middle and upper sequence, respectively; locally may contain coarse proximal turbidites	Sand and shale deposited by turbidity flow in submarine fans; hemipelagic terrigenous/ calcareous clays; pelagic oozes; locally proximal turbidites
Geometry and structure	Sheet-like or tabular; uniform subsidence during deposition; periodic tilting and erosion; deposited near basinal hinge-line during subsidence and/or sea level rise	Wedge-shaped lens; may be fan-shaped or lobate in plan view; slow subsidence	Elongate; lens-shaped in transverse section; may bifurcate updip; pinches out updip; slow subsidence	Variable lens-shaped; commonly irregular; reflects bathymetric configuration of structural depression; slow to rapid subsidence
Lateral relationships	Pinches out landward; grades basinward into lower delta plain, distal fan-delta, or shelf/ platform facies; may grade laterally into marine embayment facies	Pinches out updip; grades basinward into basinal plain or hemipelagic drape facies; continuous laterally for tens of kilometers	Pinches out updip and laterally; grades downdip into continental rise, mounded turbidites, or large submarine fans	Pinches out in every direction
Nature of upper/lower boundaries	Upper surface commonly tilted, eroded, and onlapped by similar deposits; base of facies onlaps unconformity, commonly angular	Upper surface commonly baselapped by prograding clinoforms; basal surface onlaps updip against eroded slope (and commonly outer shelf); may show baselap basinward against mounds or bathymetric highs	Upper surface may be concordant with overlying shelf or platform reflections or commonly baselapped by prograding prodelta and slope facies; basal surface onlaps updip and laterally; baselap onto basin floor rarely observed	Upper surface may be concordant with hemipelagic drape or baselapped by prograding clinoforms; basal surface onlaps in all directions
Amplitude	Variable; locally high but normally low to moderate	Variable; hemipelagic facies moderate to high; clastics low to moderate	Variable; generally low to moderate	Variable; generally low to moderate
Continuity	Low in clastics; higher in carbonate facies; decreases landward	Moderate to high; continuous reflections in response to hemipelagic facies	Variable; generally low to moderate	Variable; poor in chaotic or mounded fill; high in low-density turbidites and hemipelagics
Frequency (cycle breadth)	Variable; generally moderate to narrow	Narrow; uniform	Variable but generally narrow	Variable; commonly narrow; may increase breadth toward axis of fill

*Modified from Vail et al. (1977, pp. 160-168); changes by Brown and Fisher.

A variety of baselap terminations, and hence, unconformities, occur on seismic profiles illustrated in this chapter; for example, baselap unconformities (figs. 3, 8, 9, 13, 19, 23, 46); toplap unconformities (figs. 8, 9, 13, 19, 23, 38); and onlap unconformities (figs. 9, 19, 29, 32, 33, 34, 36, 37 38, 39, 40, 43, 49). Erosional (angular) unconformities are illustrated on figures 9, 19, 48, 49, 50, among others. The reader can refer to figures 10, 11, 12, 46, and 47 for further explanation.

Most possible types and combinations of erosional and lapout terminations are schematically illustrated on figure 46. A heavy line representing an angular or non-depositional unconformity is shown on the figure. Presence of an actual reflection in response to the unconformity depends upon the relative density/velocity differences across the unconformity. Occurrence of a reflection coefficient from an unconformity (soil, weathering, caliche, cementation, etc.) that is higher than overlying or underlying strata will result in a continuous reflection (Vail et al., 1977). They note that dipping beds above and below an unconformity with reflection coefficients similar to the unconformity produce discontinuous reflections as a result of going in and out of phase with reflections from overlying/underlying beds. Concordant unconformities commonly exhibit density/velocity changes that produce continuous reflections. Where insufficient velocity contrast occurs across angular (erosional and/or lapout) unconformities, the discontinuity caused by uniform terminations permit the interpreter to recognize the unconformity even though it is not represented by a reflection.

Significance of the hiatus along an unconformity (fig. 47) can be estimated, and, as noted, it can be more precisely estimated if paleontological zones can be correlated from well sites. Some very complicated hiatal relationships may occur when the magnitude of the erosional hiatus trends counter to non-depositional hiatuses. Angular unconformities, however, generally represent a much greater time-gap than lapout, non-depositional hiatuses.

We have mapped the age and/or facies of strata truncated below

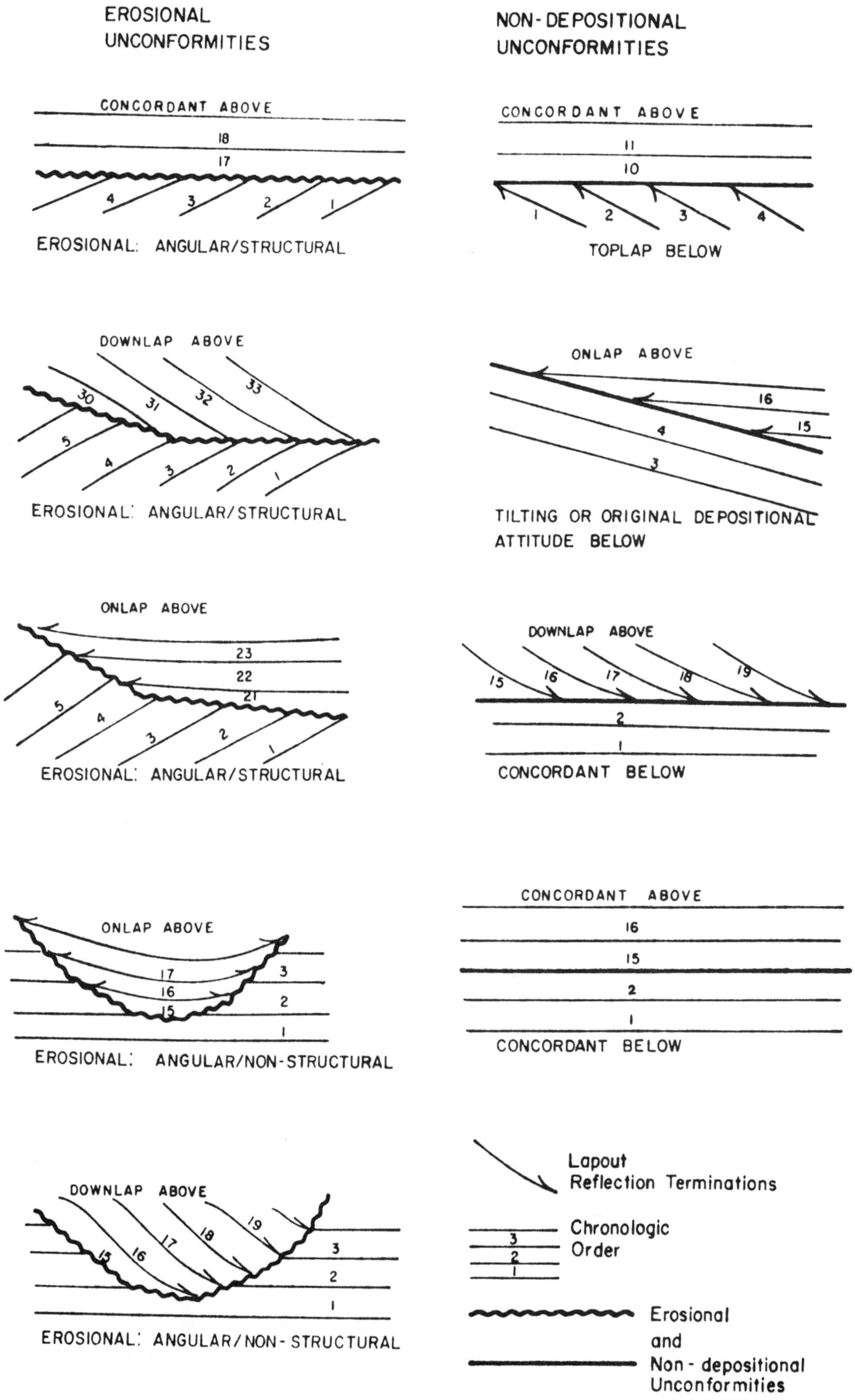

EROSIONAL
UNCONFORMITIES

NON-DEPOSITIONAL
UNCONFORMITIES

CONCORDANT ABOVE

18

17

4   3   2   1

EROSIONAL: ANGULAR/STRUCTURAL

CONCORDANT ABOVE

11

10

1   2   3   4

TOPLAP BELOW

DOWNLAP ABOVE

30   31   32   33

5   4   3   2   1

EROSIONAL: ANGULAR/STRUCTURAL

ONLAP ABOVE

16

4

15

3

TILTING OR ORIGINAL DEPOSITIONAL
ATTITUDE BELOW

ONLAP ABOVE

23

22

21

5   4   3   2   1

EROSIONAL: ANGULAR/STRUCTURAL

DOWNLAP ABOVE

15   16   17   18   19

2

1

CONCORDANT BELOW

ONLAP ABOVE

17   3

16   2

15   1

EROSIONAL: ANGULAR/NON-STRUCTURAL

CONCORDANT ABOVE

16

15

2

1

CONCORDANT BELOW

DOWNLAP ABOVE

15   16   17   18   19

3

2

1

EROSIONAL: ANGULAR/NON-STRUCTURAL

Lapout
Reflection Terminations

3
2   Chronologic
1   Order

Erosional
and
Non-depositional
Unconformities

Figure 46. Seismic reflection configurations that define unconformities.

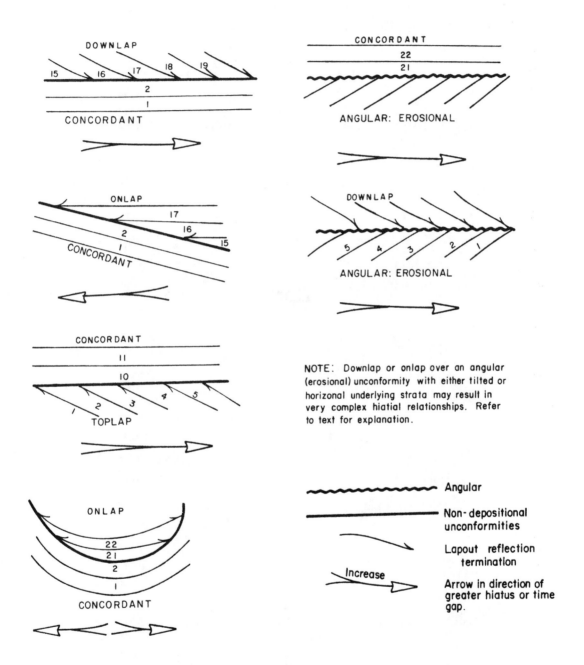

Figure 47. Inferring the relative magnitude of a hiatus using seismic reflection configurations.

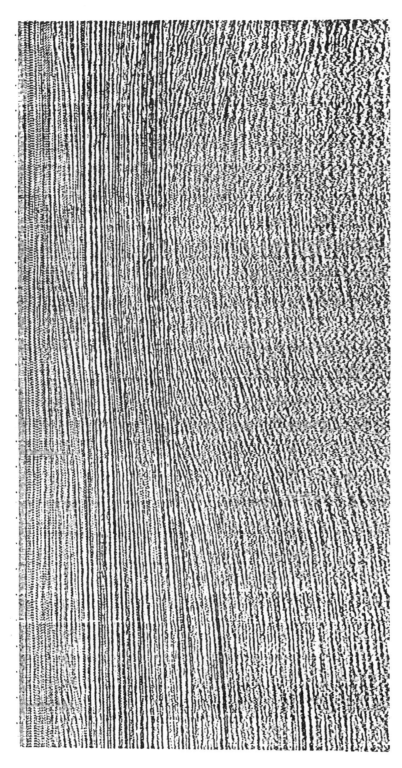

Figure 48. Eroded structure along U. S. Geologic Survey seismic profile, Baltimore Canyon area, offshore U. S. Atlantic. From Dobrin (1978), AAPG Seismic Stratigraphy course notes.

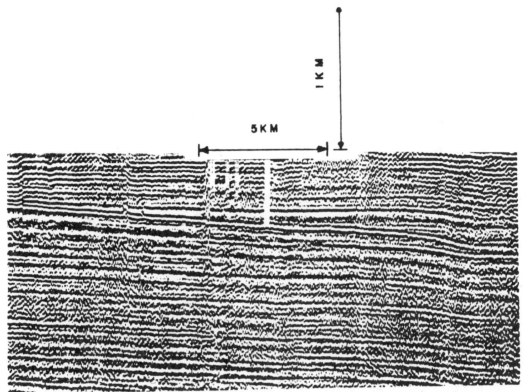

Figure 49. Erosional unconformity overlain by onlap seismic facies Gulf of Mexico. From Dobrin (1977) after Kendall (1967).

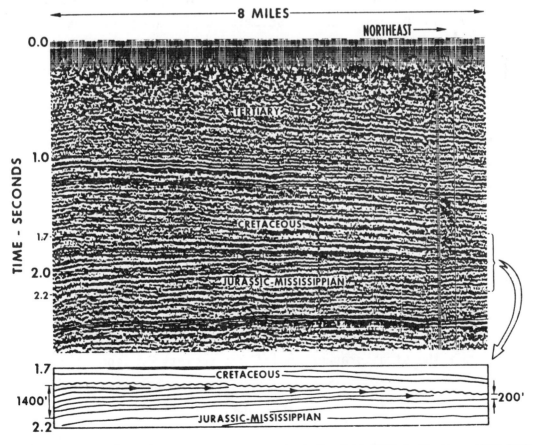

Figure 50. Prudhoe Bay oil field showing regional pre-Cretaceous unconformity. From Dobrin (1977) after Morgridge and Smith (1972).

angular unconformities. Such "subcrop" maps may be useful, for example, in determining areal relationship between eroded reservoir facies and younger onlapping seal/source beds. Likewise, the nature of facies that lap out against an unconformity may permit reconstruction of subaerial exposure and erosion history necessary to produce favorable, leached diagenetic porosity.

Unconformity analysis is important to complete the tectonic and structural history of a basin. Seal and source may be associated with unconformities. Also, understanding the burial and uplift/erosional history of strata during basinal evolution requires careful study and mapping of unconformities--local and regional.

Summary

Vail et al. (1977) have introduced new terminology and new concepts that are most useful in seismic facies interpretation. Descriptive terminology involves three types: reflection terminations, reflection configurations, and external form of geometry of seismic facies (fig. 51). Most of the nomenclature is geometric and descriptive. Use of the basic concepts of seismic sequence and seismic facies analysis, however, depends to a great extent on the interpreter's experience in depositional processes, environments and facies. We emphasize the need for understanding both modern geophysical and modern genetic stratigraphic concepts. Stratigraphic interpretation of modern seismic profiles requires the interpreter to think in terms of dynamic depositional processes if maximum use is to be made of these concepts.

Benefits from stratigraphic interpretation using seismic data are many. It provides continuous and precisely correlated data that cannot be obtained with well data. Discontinuities by erosion and non-deposition, as well as depositional surfaces, can be recognized and mapped throughout a basin. Pinchout, thinning/thickening, and erosion of beds can be inferred directly from the seismic profile. Paleontologic zones can be traced along isochronous reflections. Configurations of reflections permit the stratigrapher to infer a variety of depositional processes and paleoslopes. Structural activity can be integrated easily with the stratigraphic record. The capability of mapping a great

REFLECTION TERMINATIONS (AT SEQUENCE BOUNDARIES)	REFLECTION CONFIGURATIONS (WITHIN SEQUENCES)	EXTERNAL FORMS (OF SEQUENCES AND SEISMIC FACIES UNITS)
LAPOUT	PRINCIPAL STRATAL CONFIGURATION	
BASELAP	PARALLEL	SHEET
ONLAP	SUBPARALLEL	SHEET DRAPE
DOWNLAP	DIVERGENT	WEDGE
TOPLAP	PROGRADING CLINOFORMS	BANK
TRUNCATION	SIGMOID	LENS
EROSIONAL	OBLIQUE	MOUND
STRUCTURAL	COMPLEX SIGMOID-OBLIQUE	FILL
CONCORDANCE	SHINGLED	
(NO TERMINATION)	HUMMOCKY CLINOFORM	
	CHAOTIC	
	REFLECTION-FREE	
	MODIFYING TERMS	

EVEN	HUMMOCKY
WAVY	LENTICULAR
REGULAR	DISRUPTED
IRREGULAR	CONTORTED
UNIFORM	
VARIABLE	

Figure 51. Terminology proposed by Exxon explorationists to describe reflection terminations, reflection configurations, and geometry of seismic facies. From Mitchum et al. (1977).

variety of stratigraphic features, depositional processes, and inferred lithofacies increases the stratigrapher's capability by an order of magnitude.

FACTORS CONTROLLING DEPOSITION OF CYCLIC SEQUENCES

Some of the more recurring questions in stratigraphic analysis involve statisfactory explanations for repetitive depositional sequences in basin fills. As such repetitive sequences are readily observable on seismic profiles they take on particular focus in seismic stratigraphic analyses. Vail et al. (1977) present a cogent, well-reasoned, and well-structured series of models to explain their observations. Very simply, they integrate occurrences of coastal onlap, marine (deep-water) onlap, baselap and toplap into an elaborate model which involves asymmetric cyclic oscillations of relative sea level. They define a relative change as apparent rise or fall of sea level with respect to the land surface, which may be caused by rise or fall of sea level, the land surface, or both in combination (Vail et al., 1977, p. 63). They recognize local, regional and global cycles of relative sea level change. The cycle of relative change of sea level is defined as the interval of time occupied by a relative rise and fall of sea level.

A *cycle* of relative rise or fall of sea level (Vail et al., 1977) is inferred to consist of gradual relative rise, a period of stillstand and a rapid relative fall of sea level. The total gradual rise is inferred to consist of several smaller scale, rapid rises and stillstands; they call this a *paracycle*. According to their observations and models, several relative cycles exhibit successive rises to higher relative sea level positions followed by one or more major relative falls to a lower position. This higher order cycle is called a *supercycle*.

Although Vail et al. (1977) carefully state that some cycles may be local or perhaps of regional extent, the implication throughout their papers is that cycles *are* of global significance. They state that most regional cycles are eventually determined to be global in extent and that "simultaneous relative changes in three or more widely spaced regions around the globe are interpreted as global changes of sea level" (idem., p. 63). Finally, even the collective title of their papers in Memoir 26 (American Association of Petroleum Geologists) is "Seismic Stratigraphy and *Global* (our italics) Changes of Sea Levels." Consequently, in all candor, their models for explaining cyclic sequences should be viewed as models controlled principally by absolute or eustatic sea level changes. To think otherwise may prove confusing when the reader reviews their concepts. We conclude that their ultimate explanation for most cyclic sequences implies a eustatic control and, despite the use of "relative sea level changes," their model implies that eustatic rates are assumed to be consistently greater than basin subsidence rates. We disagree with this basic premise as does Pitman (1978).

We have observed independently on seismic profiles almost every feature described by Vail et al. (1977). In addition, we generally use the same criteria for recognizing seismic sequences and for interpreting seismic facies. Nevertheless, we differ on several points which are critical in their eustatic sea level model.

Evidence of Sea Level Changes (Vail et al., 1977)

According to Vail et al. (1977), indicators of relative sea level changes can be grouped into three basic lines of evidence: (1) coastal onlap indicates a relative rise; (2) coastal toplap indicates stillstand; and (3) downward shift in coastal onlap indicates a relative (rapid) fall of sea level.

Coastal onlap (fig. 36) as we previously noted is the progressive landward termination of reflections from coastal (paralic) lithofacies. Vail et al. note that coastal onlap may be caused by one of the following: (1) rising sea level when the basin subsides, remains stationary or rises at a slower rate than sea level; (2) sea level remains stationary and the basin subsides; and (3) sea level falls, but subsidence occurs at a greater rate. We earlier noted that beach or shoreline facies rarely onlap against subaerially eroded strata. Rather, delta plain or lower alluvial plain facies commonly onlap the coastal unconformity, introducing a few meters of error in marking maximum relative sea level.

Figure 36 exhibits coastal onlap of more than 4 seconds from Jurassic to Late Cretaceous. Unless one wishes to infer several thousand feet of sea level rise, it is necessary to assume that sea level rise and basin subsidence (plus sediment compaction) are responsible for the gross amount of coastal onlap. A schematic model (fig. 52) illustrates this concept.

A significant point made by Vail et al. (1977) is the general belief that relative sea level rise necessarily produces a shoreline transgression. Figure 53 schematically illustrates an accepted stratigraphic pattern recognized in basins such as the Gulf Coast basin (Lowman, 1949). In the example, one can see that a shoreline shift during a relative sea level (coastal onlap) rise is a function of sea level change, subsidence and sediment supply. Three scenarios are possible during coastal onlap (fig. 54): shoreline transgression, regression or stationary. These three patterns have been recognized in ancient basins. Determining eustatic sea level rise using coastal onlap must involve adjustment for subsidence and sediment compaction. If these factors can be approximated, then subtraction from the total coastal aggradation will result in a valid eustatic value.

Coastal toplap has been discussed and is exhibited on a number of profiles (figs. 8, 9, 13, 19, 23, 46). According to Vail et al. (1977), toplap is indicative of a stillstand of relative sea level. It infers that basin subsidence and absolute sea level remain essentially stationary during a period of progradation. Because toplap, by definition, results from oblique progradation, one can infer that progradation is probably rapid and under the influence of deltaic deposition. Toplap occurs because deltaic or other prograding coastal systems cannot aggrade more than a few meters above sea level, thus requiring a basinward shift in nearshore depositional environments. Rate of progradation will be controlled by sediment supply, depth of water and stability of sea level subsidence. A schematic diagram illustrates the development of toplap (fig. 55).

Downward shift in coastal onlap according to Vail et al. (1977) indicates a relative (and rapid) fall in sea level. They note that it can occur if (1) absolute sea level falls while the basin floor is uplifted, remains stationary or subsides at a lower rate than sea level change; (2) if sea level remains stationary while the basin floor is uplifted; or (3) if sea level rises but the basin floor is uplifted at a greater rate. Downward shift in coastal onlap is measured from the highest position of

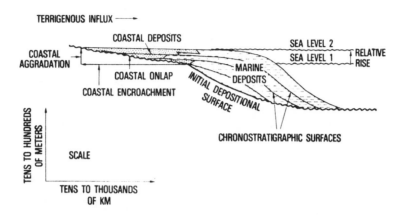

Figure 52. Coastal onlap indicates a relative rise of sea level. From Vail et al. (1977).

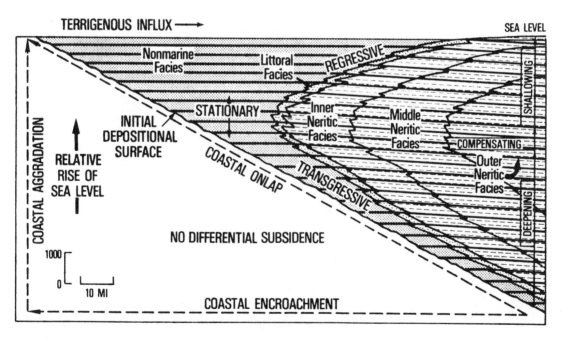

Figure 53. Coastal onlap contemporaneous with marine (shoreline) transgression and regression. From Vail et al. (1977).

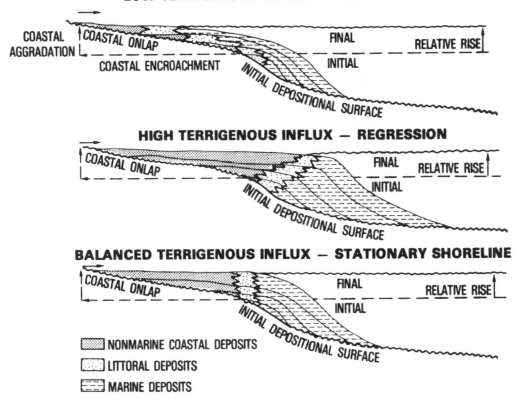

Figure 54. Transgression, regression and coastal onlap during relative rise of sea level. From Vail et al. (1977).

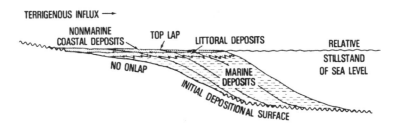

Figure 55. Coastal toplap indicates a relative stillstand of sea level. From Vail et al. (1977).

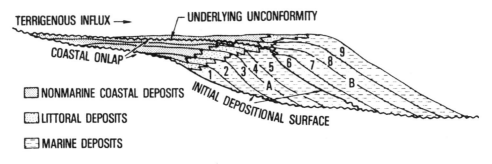

Figure 56. Downward shift in coastal onlap indicates relative fall of sea level. From Vail et al. (1977).

onlap termination in one sequence to the termination of the next super-posed sequence. Figure 56 illustrates the principle of "downward shift in coastal onlap."

Vail et al. (1977) illustrate downward shift in coastal onlap with a line from the San Joaquin basin (fig. 57). They verify by well data that the Santa Margarita is a coastal deposit rather than a marine onlap deposit. We have personally observed one probable example of downward shift in coastal onlap below a shelf edge not associated with marine on-lap. We have observed several "downward shifts" in proximal areas where slight fall in relative sea level may shift a coastline basinward.

Other examples by Vail et al. (1977) are to us less convincing. They illustrate two examples of "downward shift" from the North Sea, one of which is included in this chapter (fig. 58). The parts of these seismic profiles illustrated do not indicate to us a downward shift in coastal onlap, but rather illustrate examples of alternating progradational (down-lapping) clinoforms and onlapping deep-marine facies (our continental rise onlap). Perhaps downward shift can be documented landward of these pro-file segments. Nevertheless, we have observed many examples exactly like the North Sea examples from several basins (and several oceans) without yet recognizing associated downward shift in coastal onlap below the shelf edge (or even to a position on the outer shelf). We admit that we may have failed to recognize "downward shift," but until we do, we remain uncon-vinced of its pervasive occurrence in every cyclic sequence in the world. Therefore, we are not convinced that it necessarily follows that marine onlap always indicates a downward shift in coastal onlap. We cannot call marine onlap "lowstand" deposits without direct evidence of contemporane-ous downward shift in coastal onlap. In addition, we are not convinced that one or one hundred "downward shift" examples necessarily prove that all marine onlaps are "low stand" deposits. We are concerned that Vail et al. (1977) infer that marine-onlaps are cause and effect proof of sea level fall, even when downward shift cannot be observed. It seems to us that it may be circuitous reasoning to assume that all marine onlaps are represented somewhere by downward shift in coastal environments below a shelf edge. Unless there is direct evidence of coincident "downward shift" and marine onlap, we are not now prepared to use marine onlap alone as

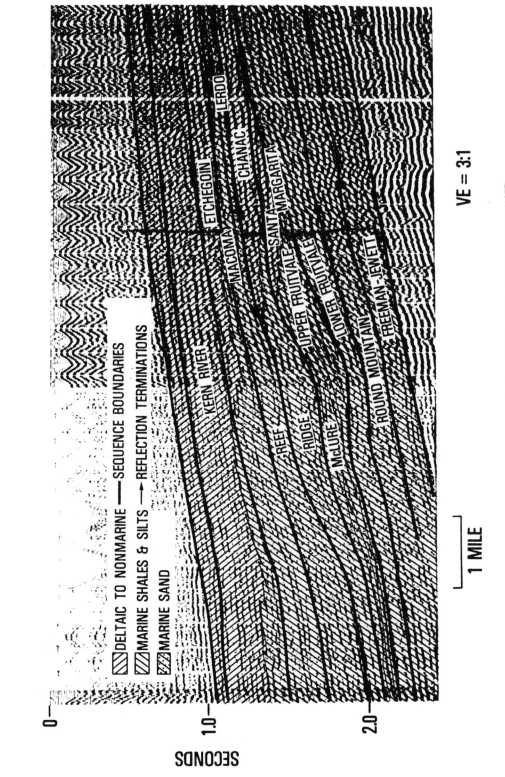

Figure 57. Downward shift in coastal onlap, San Joaquin basin, California. From Vail et al. (1977).

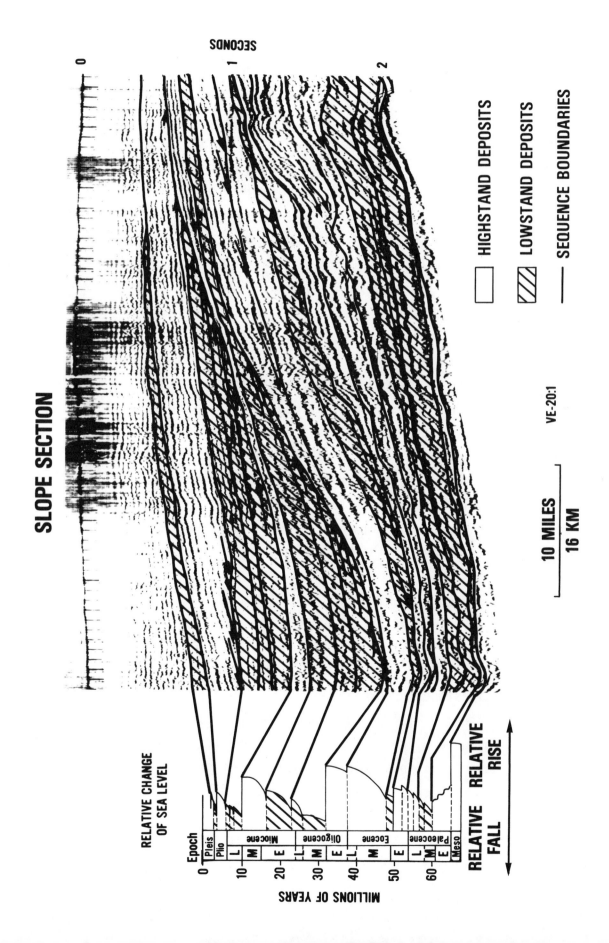

Figure 58. Progradational and marine onlap cycles. Tertiary, North Sea basin. From Vail et al. (1977).

evidence of low stand deposition.

Vail et al. (1977) illustrate their method of calculating the amount
of downward shift as a measurement of sea level fall (fig. 59), as well
as the amount of coastal onlap (and coastal aggradation) as a measurement of subsequent sea level rise. Construction of charts showing inferred changes in sea level is explained thoroughly and the reader is referred to those procedures (idem, p. 77-81; 83-97). The hierarchy of sea
level charts showing the relationship of paracycle, cycle and supercycle
is illustrated by figure 60.

Conceptual models presented by Vail et al. (1977) illustrate their
conclusions regarding the deposition of cycle sequences (fig. 61). We
verify the marine offlap phase of their model, although we do not necessarily attribute associated coastal onlap to global rises in sea level.
The marine onlap phase of their model does not agree with our current
experience. As previously mentioned, we have observed one case of downward shift of coastal onlap below a shelf edge and it clearly was related
to uplift of a fault block. The scores of marine onlap sequences that
we have observed have yet to be correlated with "downward shift." However, it is difficult to challenge their conclusion that global cycles
exist because the fundamental evidence depends upon the precision of
paleontologic correlations of these sequences.

INFERRED SEA LEVEL EVENTS CONTROLLING
ORIGIN OF CYCLIC SEQUENCES
(Vail et al., 1977)

1. Stillstand: progradation
3. Gradually rising sea level: marine onlap
   followed by coastal onlap
2. Rapid fall in sea level: exposure of shelf
   and erosion of river valleys below shelf edge
   (downward shift in coastal onlap)
1. Stillstand: progradation of coastal systems
   and/or shelf edge, slope (marine) offlap

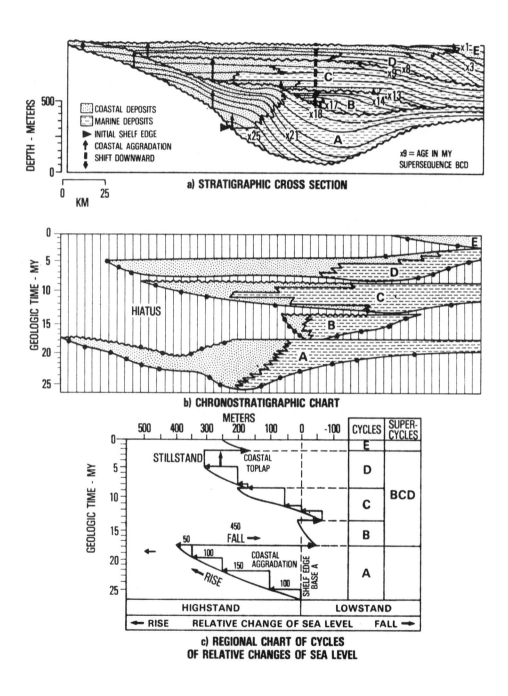

Figure 59. Procedure for constructing regional chart of cycles of relative changes of sea level. From Vail et al. (1977).

In pre-glacial sequences, we have not observed incised river valleys across a shelf. We recognize the coincidence of slope and outer shelf canyons with occurrence of marine onlap sequences. The canyons, however, are not river valleys of the Pleistocene variety, but are deep (up to 2200 meters), wide (several tens of kilometers at shelf edge), may bifurcate updip, and always disappear updip into uneroded shelf deposits. We have yet to recognize fluvial or estuarine facies within the canyons, as are typical of most drowned Pleistocene river valleys that underlie continental shelf areas. Only turbidites, hemipelagics and deep neritic facies have been penetrated in canyons that we have studied. We have not been able to correlate a river or delta system with an onlap rise. In fact, some of the deepest canyons that we have mapped are eroded into thick carbonate platforms with no evidence of fluvial or deltaic deposits in the platform sequence. Furthermore, the youngest strata eroded by every canyon that we have observed either on seismic profiles or using conventional subsurface data, represent maximum marine transgression of the shelf (commonly carbonates or biogenics). We acknowledge, however, that a river valley or shelf-edge subaerial canyon eroded during a "downward shift" might be kept open and enlarged by submarine processes during subsequent sea level rise and transgression.

If one assumes a single, global control of cyclic sequences, then one has the option to devise many depositional scenarios. This is especially true when control is assumed to be something so pervasive as absolute sea level. We are not convinced that the world's stratigraphic sequences are the result of a single unifying control that normally overrides all intrabasinal factors. It is difficult for us to understand what natural phenomena combined to insure that global sea level, controlled by the world's total oceanic volume, would fall exactly the prescribed amount and rate during *every* cycle to produce an asymmetric shift in sea level required to place a shoreline *precisely* below the shelf edge in order to deposit a marine onlap sequence. This coincidence is particularly suspicious in view of Pitman's (1978) contention that eustatic sea level changes (which we all know occur) are of insufficient rates to drop sea level below a shelf edge in a basin undergoing normal rates of subsidence. At this time we choose to consider that cyclic sequences may be controlled

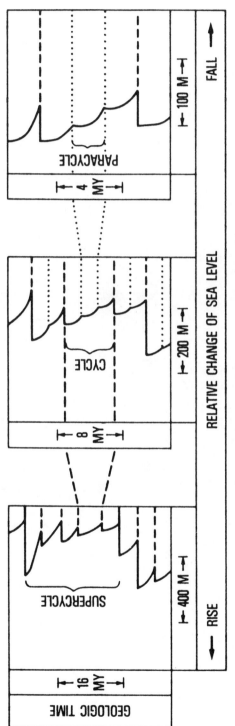

Figure 60. Charts of relative changes in sea level. Shows concept of paracycles, cycles and supercycles. From Vail et al. (1977).

100

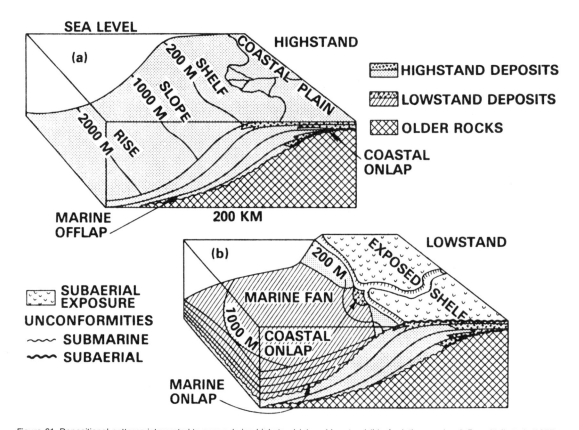

Figure 61. Depositional patterns interpreted to occur during highstand (a) and lowstand (b) of relative sea level. From Vail et al. (1977).

by an interplay among basin subsidence, shelf tilting, sediment rates and eustatic changes in sea level that is much more complex than a single, global factor.

Figure 62 shows abrupt falls in sea level which apparently correlate exactly. Is the precision of paleontologic correlations really this absolute? What causes up to 400 meters (fig. 63) of rapid fall of absolute sea level? Should such sea level oscillations suddenly fall more than 350 meters lower than Pitman's (1978) calculated sea level which Vail et al. (1977) used to calibrate their own sea level charts? The closest apparent correlation of "global" cycles in figure 62 is between the North Sea and northwest Africa; these two regions also are inferred to correlate closely with the Gulf of Mexico basin (idem, p. 145-163). Did these basins experience similar tectonic and consequently, depositional events during their post-rift development? What about their correlation (fig. 62) with the Gippsland Basin of Australia or the San Joaquin Basin of California? We remain skeptical of absolute global correlation of cyclic events of this scale and precision. Consequently more documentation will be required to convince us that asymmetric eustatic sea level oscillations continually and almost exclusively overrode basin tectonics and sedimentation rates to produce contemporaneous global sequences in all of the world's basins.

Some Questions About Eustatic Control of Cyclic Sequences

1) Downward shift in coastal onlap below shelf edge is required for every cycle? How common is "downward shift" below shelf edge? Can it be documented for most marine onlap cycles?

2) Marine onlap may occur by submarine erosion/transport processes without direct coastal source of sediment?

3) Canyons that eroded shelf and slope systems may be several thousand meters deep and tens of kilometers wide at shelf edge. Are these river valleys?

4) Canyons disappear and may bifurcate updip into eroded shelf. Why do they not connect with river valleys?

5) Why are fluvial or estuarine facies absent in canyons?

6) Are sudden falls in sea level up to 400 meters (and 350 meters from

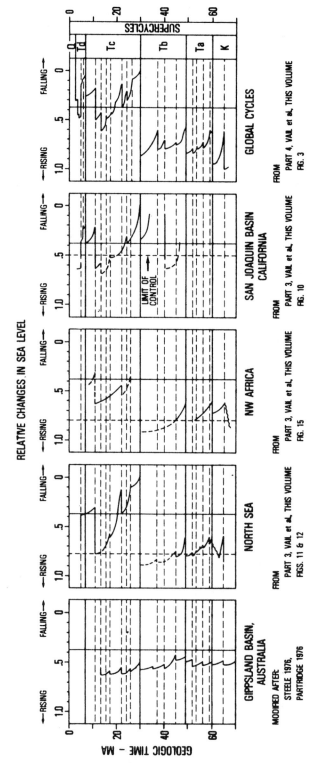

Figure 62. Correlation of regional cycles of relative sea level change and averaging to construct global cycles. From Vail et al. (1977).

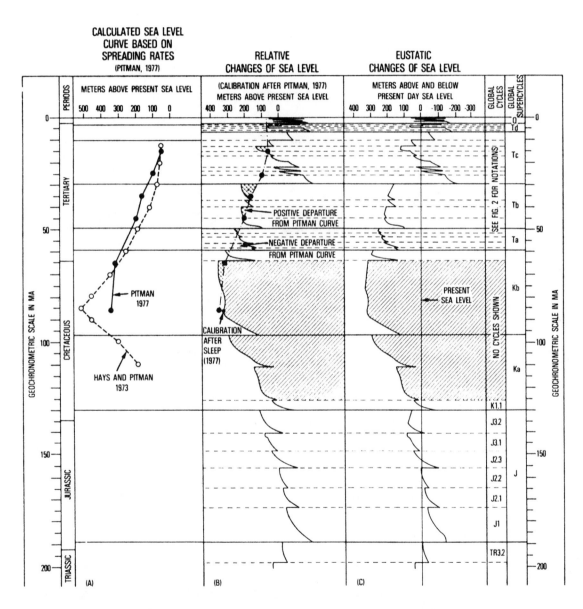

Figure 63. Estimation of eustatic changes from Jurassic to Holocene. From Vail et al. (1977).

calculated eustatic curves, of Pitman, 1978) reasonable?

7) What global phenomenon in the ocean basins can produce a score of post-rift cycles that are all asymmetric and all of approximately the same magnitude?

8) How correlative are Atlantic margin global charts with those of other basins with different tectonic styles? Has there been sufficient sampling to verify global correlation?

9) If most regional cycles are global, then must we assume that the world's basins rarely exhibit tectonic activity at sufficient rates to override eustatic sea level changes?

10) A shelf-edge and slope are inferred to change abruptly from progradational deposition to marine onlap deposition in response to a downward shift in coastal onlap? The unconformity at the base of the marine onlap should be essentially non-depositional, but we find them to be highly erosional and angular throughout the basin margin.

Alternative Ideas About Cyclic Sequences

Except for the origin of marine onlap and associated canyons, we generally concur with the seismic stratigraphic concepts of Vail and his associates. The correct interpretation of the origin of marine onlap is more than an academic question. It is a question that can affect concepts of exploration for deep-water reservoirs.

In review, the model by Vail et al. (1977) requires downward shift in coastal onlap produced by a rapid fall in sea level to produce river incision across the shelf and to place a delta on the upper slope. Sediments from the river mouth are funneled down the slope *via* erosional canyons to produce onlapping submarine fans. As sea level gradually rises, the delta "retreats" up the valley and the marine onlap shifts up the slope in response. Delta sediments continue to pour down the submerged valley *via* turbidity flow eroding relict shelf sediments and depositing them and the river sediments in the marine onlap environment (continental rise). Marine onlap facies are, therefore, inferred to be composed of directly fed river sediment mixed with relict sediment eroded by turbidity currents.

What difference does it make how marine onlap is deposited? Several reasons: (1) In our experience most submarine fan reservoirs occur in onlap slope systems; (2) There appears to be a valid relationship between reservoir composition/quality and the nature of relict sediments eroded by submarine canyons on the shelf; and, (3) We have rarely observed productive submarine fan reservoirs in prograding, river-fed slope systems. Consequently, we believe that trap potential and reservoir quality are best in onlapping submarine fans rather than offlapping fans. Reservoir quality is closely tied to a relict sediment source on the shelf rather than to a direct river-fed source.

Models presented by Vail et al. (1977) infer that all sediment deposited in deep-water is introduced by direct river/delta depositon. We believe that much turbidity deposition in basins results from reworked relict slope and shelf sediment. This conclusion is important in deep-water reservoir prospecting. We will present alternative models to explain deep-water deposition and facies. These ideas are not without problems, but we believe that the full story of deep-water sedimentation is not limited to direct feeding by coastal systems. We will limit our consideration principally to seismic-stratigraphic evidence of deep-water deposition.

Review of seismic profiles from a variety of basins of the world shows that several fundamental types of slope systems exist (fig. 64). Within modern and ancient basins, an interpreter can recognize seismic reflections that infer offlap or basinward accretion of slope sediment requiring introduction of a relatively sustained sediment supply from the shelf that overrides the effects of sea level rise and/or basin subsidence (fig. 64A). Submarine fans on a prograding slope are buried by subsequent fans to produce the characteristic offlap clinoforms. In other basins with active contemporaneous tectonism, submarine fans are deposited in a superposed sequence identified as onlap fill or what we have called uplap systems (fig. 64C, D). Sediment introduced into these rapidly subsiding basins is unable to prograde and, hence, onlap fill or uplap superposition occurs. Most ancient and modern basins exhibit some variety of marine onlap (fig. 64B) which commonly laps shelfward over eroded slope or outer shelf facies. Submarine fans in an onlap slope

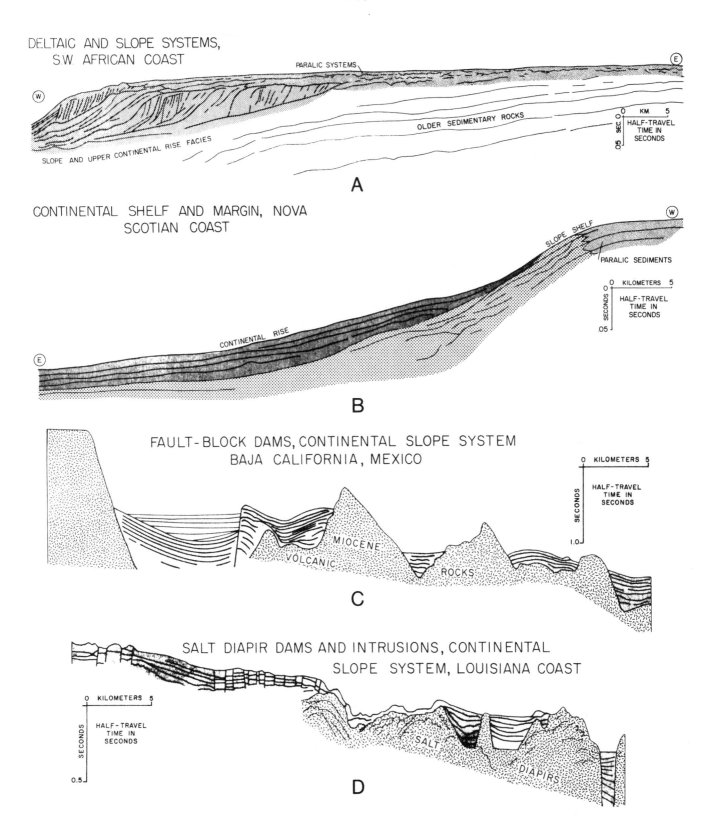

DELTAIC AND SLOPE SYSTEMS,
S.W. AFRICAN COAST

A

CONTINENTAL SHELF AND MARGIN, NOVA
SCOTIAN COAST

B

FAULT-BLOCK DAMS, CONTINENTAL SLOPE SYSTEM
BAJA CALIFORNIA, MEXICO

C

SALT DIAPIR DAMS AND INTRUSIONS, CONTINENTAL
SLOPE SYSTEM, LOUISIANA COAST

D

Figure 64. Nature of seismic reflections that characterize several styles of deposition along some Holocene contenental margins. From Brown and Fisher, 1977, after McMaster et al., 1970 (A); Uchupi and Emergy, 1967 (B); Emery, 1970 (C); and Uchupi and Emery, 1968.

system shift shelfward, indicating a retreating source. Vail et al. (1977) explain the shelfward onlap by rising sea level and "retreating" deltas. Onlap slope deposits may vary from widespread, enormously thick continental rise deposits that extend hundreds of kilometers along eroded slopes to localized fan deposits at the mouth of small submarine canyons. In each case, however, they onlap erosional unconformities. We infer that evidence from modern oceans (fig. 65) and from ancient basins (fig. 66) indicates that most, if not all, of the slope sediment in onlap systems is derived by submarine erosion of slope/shelf areas (fig. 67). (An exception is canyons that erode narrow shelves to tap nearshore marine sediment.) As the slope and outer shelf retreat by erosion (as shown by truncated reflections), the submarine fans shift landward in response to this retreating, diminishing sediment supply.

We recognize from seismic data, therefore, two principal types of slope systems (excluding the structurally active basins): offlapping or prograding slopes and onlapping or retreating slopes (figs. 67, 68). We call these constructive and destructive slopes, respectively.

CONSTRUCTIVE SLOPES

° *Offlap (progradational):*
Deposition > subsidence
(or relative rise in sea level)
° *Uplap (superposed or onlap-fill):*
Deposition $\cong$ tectonic or salt subsidence
(or relative rise in sea level)

DESTRUCTIVE SLOPES

° *Onlap (marine onlap or rise):*
Deposition < subsidence
(or relative rise in sea level)

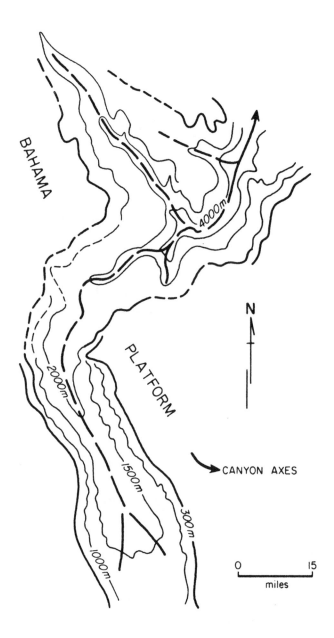

Figure 65. Tongue of the Ocean, a submarine canyon eroded into the Bahama Platform. From Shepard (1973).

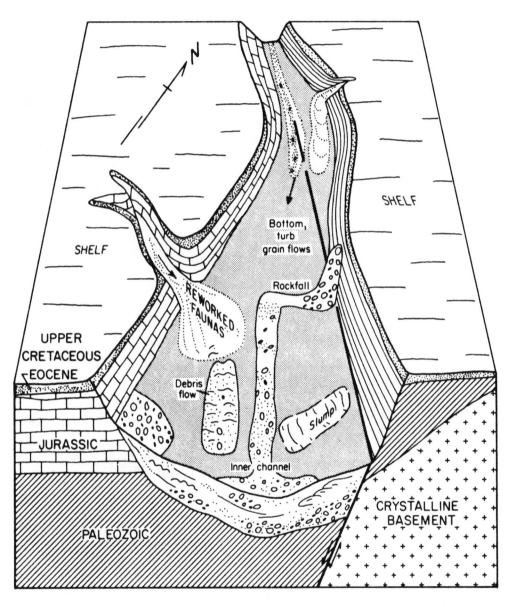

Figure 66. Major submarine canyon eroded more than 1000 m into pre-Cenozoic strata and filled during Eocene and Oligocene. From Picha (1979).

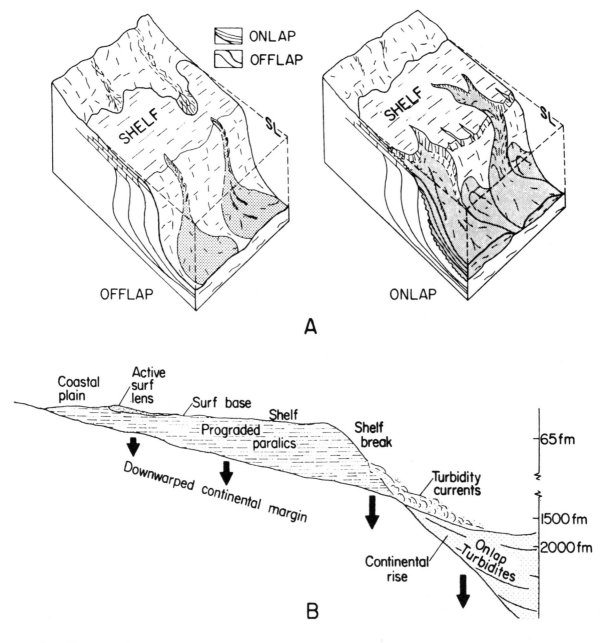

Figure 67. Nature of offlap and onlap slope deposition. From Brown and Fisher (1977). Onlap processes diagram (B). After Dietz (1963).

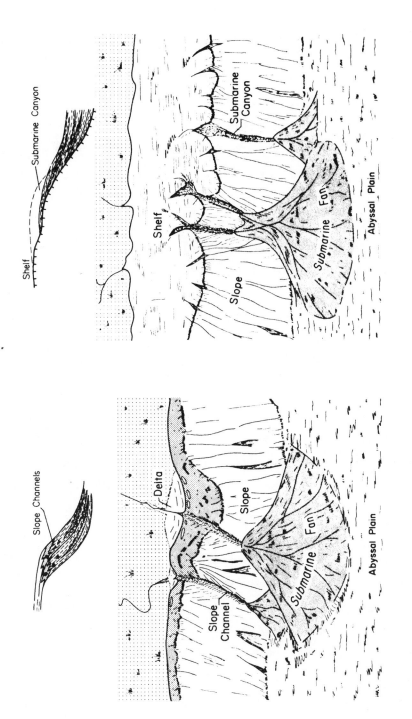

Figure 68. Constructive slope with active shelf-margin delta and destructive slope with extensive erosion. Modified from Moore and Asquith (1971).

Conceptually, each of these slope models (fig. 69) can be recognized on seismic facies that previously have been described. These generalized models are not expected to represent the myriad variations possible under combinations of structural setting and sediment source, but we believe that they may serve to open up a dialog among interpreters who are "thinking processes" when they analyze seismic profiles. We also think that these depositional scenarios are compatible with current sedimentary process concepts. Our approach goes beyond most "turbidite" models, however, by (1) introducing the element of internal configuration of stratal surfaces, (2) viewing turbidites and submarine fans as systems that are spatially arranged within basins by long-term tectonic influence and sedimentary processes, and (3) providing an approach (seismic stratigraphic) for prospecting these deeply buried systems with limited well or outcrop data. During the evolution of ancient basins, each type of slope model may operate, alternate, or evolve into another. In Brazilian basins, for example, we have observed rift basin slope systems (fig. 69-IV) that evolved into carbonate slope systems (fig. 69-IV), which in turn evolved into onlap slope systems (fig. 69-III) followed by offlap slope systems (fig. 69-II), which alternated periodically with short-term onlap slope deposition (fig. 69-III).

We believe that it would be profitable to consider other possible sea level scenarios. For example, our observations would be satisfied by a model involving an interplay of differential rates of basin subsidence and gradual changes in absolute sea level. We believe such a model as presented by Pitman (1978) has considerable attraction and should be thoroughly evaluated.

How can we use these process-defined slope models in prospecting? First, the *stratigraphic trap potential* of onlap submarine fans is obvious (fig. 70) because the fans progressively shift landward and pinch out against an erosional slope and/or canyon floor. Distal hemipelagic facies progressively onlap and seal each fan (fig. 68). Uplap (or onlap fill) submarine fans pinchout similarly against the flank of the graben or salt basin to produce similar, multiple pinchout possibilities. Care should be exercised in prospecting uplap (onlap fill) fans, however, to avoid drilling structures that were paleobathymetric highs during deposition.

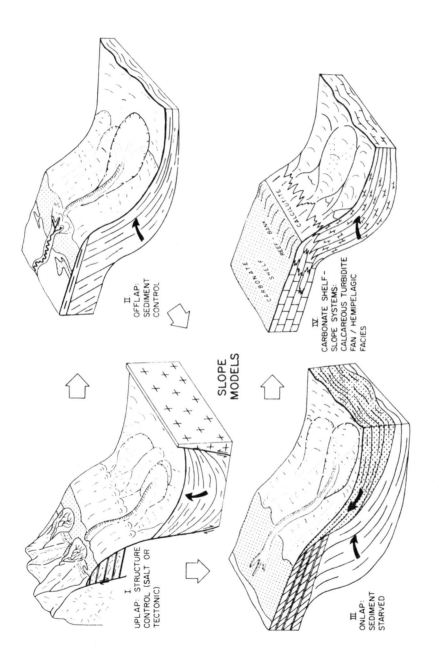

SLOPE
MODELS

I
UPLAP: STRUCTURE
CONTROL (SALT OR
TECTONIC)

II
OFFLAP: SEDIMENT
CONTROL

III
ONLAP: SEDIMENT
STARVED

IV
CARBONATE SHELF-
SLOPE SYSTEMS:
CALCAREOUS TURBIDITE
FAN / HEMIPELAGIC
FACIES

CARBONATE
SHELF

REEF- BANK

CALCILUTITE

Figure 69. Conceptual slope depositional models. Modified from Brown and Fisher (1977).

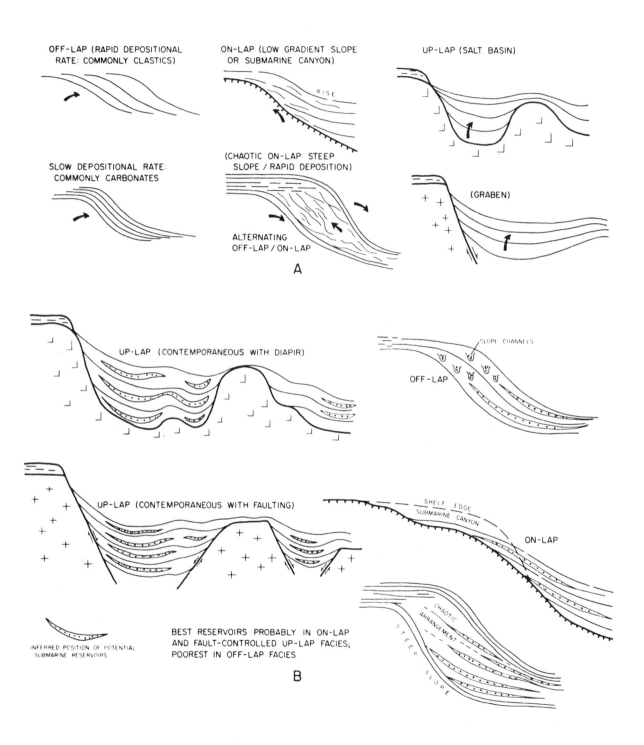

Figure 70. Seismic-stratigraphic slope reflection configurations and inferred distribution of submarine fan reservoirs. (A) Characteristic configurations and (B) Inferred sand distribution. From Brown and Fisher (1977).

Such structural or salt paleo highs may be draped by hemipelagic clays rather than turbidite sands. Offlap slopes are not high priority prospects because preservation of sand-filled feeder channels between the shelf or shelf-margin delta and submarine fan permits leaky submarine fan reservoirs*. These offlap channels (fig. 68) are eroded into the slope by downslope turbidity and grain flow from the shelf edge (Galloway and Brown, 1973). However, they do not remain open bypass conduits like onlap canyons. Rather, they shift repeatedly and the abandoned channels are sealed and preserved by further progradation, in contrast to continued slope erosion that characterizes onlap systems. Genetically, offlap slope channels resemble delta distributary channels which form by sudden channel shifting and then gradually subside and store sand.

ALTERNATE MODEL: GRADUAL EUSTATIC CHANGES
SUPERIMPOSED ON BASIN SUBSIDENCE/TILTING

2. *Gradually rising sea level (and/or basin subsidence)*: slope (marine) onlap followed by coastal onlap and extensive marine transgression; sediment starvation on outer shelf; enlargement of preexisting submarine canyons and submarine erosion of other canyons. Diminishing sea level rise (or basin subsidence) and adequate sediment supply permits initiation of progradational coastal systems over submerged shelf.

1. *Stillstand (or minimum basin subsidence)*: extensive progradation of coastal systems and/or shelf edge; slope (marine) offlap or uplap; minor submarine canyons formed at loci of shelf-edge deltas.

---

* When involved in growth-faulting, however, offlap slope sands may become traps by roll-over and fault closure.

SLOPE SYSTEMS:
DEPOSITION VS. SUBSIDENCE RATES

Sustained Sediment Supply

°   Offlap or Progradation: D > S
°   Uplap or Onlap Fill: D ≅ S

Diminishing Sediment Supply

°   Onlap or Rise: D < S

Next, how can the slope models aid in evaluation of the *reservoir quality* of submarine fans? We have inferred that slopes (fig. 69) derive their principal sediment supply in contrasting ways. We agree with Vail et al. (1977) that most prograding slope clinoforms are supplied directly by a sustained supply of shelf-margin delta sediment (fig. 71). Consequently, composition of the coastal supply (fig. 71) determines the composition (i.e., grain size, mineralogy) of offlap submarine fan systems. In addition, it is the distal fine-grained facies of coastal systems that is reworked from the shelf and carried into the basin by turbidity flow. For example, slope systems supplied by river-dominated deltas will probably be high in mud and silt and low in sand (fig. 71). Sandier delta systems generally will supply a better quality (higher sand) slope system. These delta systems normally produce oblique offlap, although in deep water, river and wave-dominated systems commonly generate growth faults and roll-over structures. We conclude, therefore, that oblique delta systems are good, sand-prone targets (Vail et al., 1977), but that slope reservoirs derived directly from delta systems during offlap *may* be sand-starved. Carbonate shelf/platform systems will generate biogenic sediment that may slowly prograde sigmoid clinoforms.

On the other hand, we believe that the principal source of onlap slope sediment is derived by slow, long-term erosion based on the magnitude of basal erosion unconformities and paleontologic dating of onlap facies (fig. 72). Therefore, we favorably view prospects in onlap submarine fans. One must determine the type of relict sediment eroded from

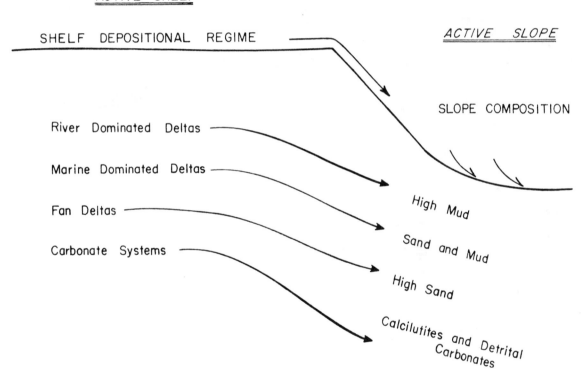

Figure 71. Probable composition of offlap on progradational slope facies supplied by various active shallow-marine systems.

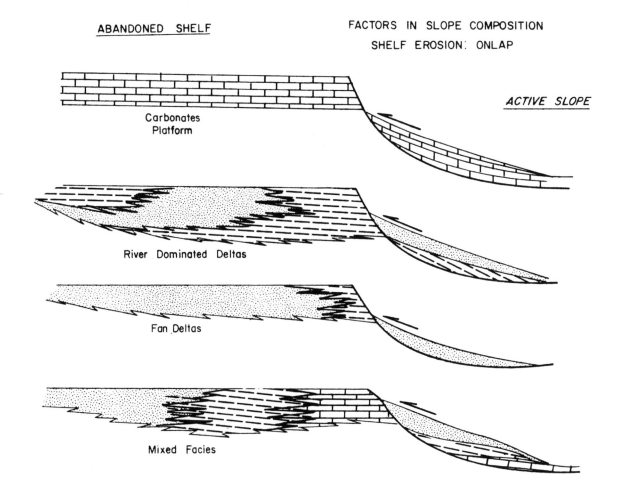

ABANDONED SHELF

FACTORS IN SLOPE COMPOSITION
SHELF EROSION: ONLAP

ACTIVE SLOPE

Carbonates
Platform

River Dominated Deltas

Fan Deltas

Mixed Facies

Figure 72. Probable composition of onlap slope facies associated with various relict shallow marine facies. This model implies a destructive, sediment starved origin for onlap slope systems.

the shelf during shelf-edge retreat and submarine canyon erosion. Obviously, the best reservoirs can be expected if a canyon taps relict sand facies. Chances are greatest when relict sandy deltas occur on the shelf. Of course, marine onlap of a carbonate platform would be composed principally of eroded limestone. Thus, we infer that the opportunity for both stratigraphic trap and reservoir potential is higher in onlap slope facies and lower in offlap slope facies.

The third type of slope system, the onlap fill or uplap slope (fig. 73), is complicated by its active structural setting. Our experience indicates that these slope systems are commonly deposited under direct feeding, although periods of erosion and canyon cutting may occur. Because structural instability dominates over sediment supply, onlap filling of subsiding salt and structural basins may occur during periods of direct feeding from the shelf, as well as when coastal supplies are diverted or absent. Structurally active basins generally possess narrow, structurally controlled shelves and nearby elevated sources. Consequently, fan deltas are common direct sources of sediments. Likewise, canyon erosion of narrow shelf areas may permit the canyon to tap nearshore sediment, a rare situation when the shelf is broad. Salt can be mobilized by any type of delta. In the Gulf of Mexico basin, river-dominated systems have generated the salt ridge/basin slope system and these basins are filled principally during periods of direct feeding and more slowly during destructional episodes. In Brazil we have observed uplap slope systems in salt basins generated by fan-delta systems. Well developed canyons are rare in slope and shelf systems associated with intensive salt tectonism, probably because erosion of extensive canyons requires long periods of stability and slope destruction. Salt basins are too mobile to permit extensive canyon erosion. To evaluate uplap reservoirs one determines the types of deltas that operated in the basin.

We have not addressed problems of porosity/permeability as a factor in reservoir quality. Nevertheless, one must evaluate this factor whether sediment is directly introduced into deep water by a coastal system or reworked during an onlap episode. Generally, fan deltas provide immature first or second-cycle sediment eroded nearby from igneous or metamorphic source rocks. For this reason, diagenetic problems may be

TECTONICALLY ACTIVE SLOPES UPLAP

FACTORS CONTROLLING SLOPE COMPOSITION:
GENERALLY DIRECT FEEDING;
MAY PERIODICALLY BECOME EROSIONAL

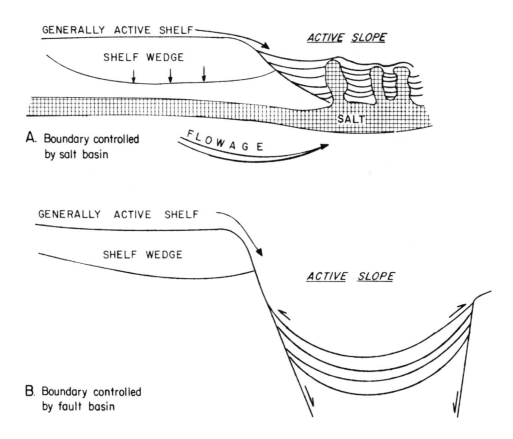

Figure 73. Factors affecting deposition in tectonically active slope/basin environments.

encountered. Deltas supplied by integrated river systems generally provide a more mature sediment. Intensity of waves and currents tends to improve the reservoir mineralogy. Of course, the burial/fluid history is a critical factor in preserving or resurrecting porosity.

Source bed quality or maturation is better satisfied, we believe, in onlap slope systems. Directly-fed river sediments are rich in terrestrial plant debris and may be gas prone source beds. On the other hand, long periods of onlap deposition during which thick hemi-pelagic and pelagic facies are deposited slowly within the basin appear to be more favorable source beds. Potential source beds are interca-lated with submarine fan sands and onlap against other eroded facies such as shelf-edge carbonates and delta sands.

CONCLUSION

Seismic-stratigraphic analysis has, we believe, already proved to be a potent approach to basin analysis. With improved geophysical and processing methods, combined with improved depositional concepts, it should become one of the principal exploration tools in the near future. Seismic modeling techniques are also adding another dimension to the use of seismic data.

Innovative, process-oriented stratigraphy must remain viable if it is to continue to contribute to this new analytical approach. More explorationists must become genetic stratigraphers, as well as seismic geophysicists, if they hope to utilize the full potential of seismic information. The field is in its infancy and it will surely change. For this change to continue to be innovative, it will require extensive publication and sharing of non-proprietary data and ideas.

REFERENCES

Asquith, D. O., 1970, Depositional topography and major marine environments, Late Cretaceous, Wyoming: AAPG Bull., v. 54, p. 1184-1224.

Bebout, D. G., and R. G. Loucks, 1974. Stuart City trend, Lower Cretaceous, South Texas--A carbonate shelf-margin model for hydrocarbon exploration: Univ. Texas, Austin, Bur. Econ. Geology Rept. Inv. 78, 80 p.

Brown, L. F., Jr., and W. L. Fisher, 1977, Seismic-stratigraphic interpretation of depositional systems: Examples from Brazilian rift and pull-apart basins, in Seismic stratigraphy--Applications to hydrocarbon exploration, C. E. Payton, ed.: AAPG Mem. 26, Tulsa, Oklahoma, 516 p., 1977, p. 213-248.

Bruce, C. H., 1973, Pressured shale and related sediment deformation: Mechanism for development of regional contemporaneous faults: AAPG Bull., v. 57, p. 878-886.

Bubb, J. N., and W. G. Hatlelid, 1977, Seismic stratigraphy and global changes of sea level, part 10: Seismic recognition of carbonate buildups, in Seismic stratigraphy--Applications to hydrocarbon exploration, C. E. Payton, ed.: AAPG Mem. 26, Tulsa, Oklahoma, 516 p., 1977, p. 185-204.

Curray, J. R., 1965, Late Quaternary history, continental shelves of the United States, in The Quaternary of the United States, Princeton Univ. Press, p. 723-735.

Dietz, R. S., 1963, Wave-base, marine profile of equilibrium, and wave-built terraces: A critical appraisal: Geol. Soc. Am. Bull., v. 74, p. 971-990.

Dobrin, M. B., 1977, Seismic Exploration for stratigraphic traps, in Seismic stratigraphy--Applications to hydrocarbon exploration, C. E. Payton, ed.: AAPG Mem. 26, Tulsa, Oklahoma, 516 p., 1977, p. 329-351.

Emery, K. O., 1970, Continental margins of the world, in The geology of the east Atlantic continental margins: Part 1. General and economic papers, F. M. Delany, ed., Rept. No. 70-13, Natural Environment Research Council, Institute of Geological Science, p. 3-29.

Galloway, W. E., and L. F. Brown, Jr., 1973, Depositional systems and shelf-slope relations on cratonic basin margin, Uppermost Pennsylvanian of North-Central Texas: AAPG Bull., v. 57, p. 1185-1218.

Heritier, F. E., Lossel, P., and Wathne, E., 1979, Trigg Field--Large submarine-fan trap in lower Eocene rocks of North Sea Viking graben: AAPG Bull., v. 63, p. 1999-2020.

Jackson, W. E., 1964, Depositional topography and cyclic deposition in west-central Texas: AAPG Bull., v. 48, p. 317-328.

Kendall, R., 1967, The role of the geophysicist in expanding man's domain: Geophysica, v. 32, p. 1-17.

McMasters, R. L., J. DeBoer, and A. Ashraf, 1970, Magnetic and seismic reflection studies on continental shelf off Portuguese Guinea, Guinea and Sierra Leone, West Africa: AAPG Bull., v. 54, p. 158-167.

Mitchum, R. M., Jr., 1977, Seismic stratigraphy and global changes in sea level, Part II: Glossary of terms used in seismic stratigraphy, in Seismic stratigraphy--Applications to hydrocarbon exploration, C. E. Payton, ed.: AAPG Mem. 26, Tulsa, Oklahoma, 516 p., 1977, p. 205-212.

_____, and P. R. Vail, Seismic stratigraphy and global changes of sea level, part 7: Seismic stratigraphic interpretation procedure, in Seismic stratigraphy--Applications to hydrocarbon exploration, C. E. Payton, ed.: AAPG Mem. 26, Tulsa, Oklahoma, 516 p., 1977, p. 135-143.

_____, P. R. Vail, and J. B. Sangree, 1977, Seismic stratigraphy and global changes of sea level, part 6: Stratigraphic interpretation of seismic reflection patterns in depositional sequences, in Seismic stratigraphy--Applications to hydrocarbon exploration, C. E. Payton, ed.: AAPG Mem. 26, Tulsa, Oklahoma, 516 p., 1977, p. 117-133.

_____, P. R. Vail, and S. Thompson, III, 1977, Seismic stratigraphy and global changes in sea level, part 2: The depositional sequence as a basic unit for seismic stratigraphic analyses, in Seismic stratigraphy--Applications to hydrocarbon exploration, C. E. Payton, ed.: AAPG Mem. 26, Tulsa, Oklahoma, 516 p., 1977, p. 53-62.

Moore, G. T., and D. O. Asquith, 1971, Delta: term and concept: Geol. Soc. Am. Bull., v. 82, p. 2563-2568.

Morgridge, D. L., and W. B. Smith, 1972, Geology and discovery of Prudhoe Bay field, eastern Arctic slope, Alaska, in Stratigraphic oil and gas fields, R. E. King, ed.: AAPG Mem. 16, p. 489-501.

Picha, F., 1979, Ancient submarine canyons of Tethyan continental margins, Czechoslovakia: AAPG Bull., v. 63, p. 67-86.

Pitman, W. C., III, 1978, Relationship between eustacy and stratigraphic sequences of passive margins: Geol. Soc. Am. Bull., v. 89, p. 1389-1403.

Rich, R. L., 1951, Three critical environments of deposition and criteria for recognition of rocks deposited in each of them: Geol. Soc. Am. Bull., v. 62, p. 1-20.

Sangree, J. B., and J. M. Widmer, 1977, Seismic stratigraphy and global changes of sea level, part 9: Seismic interpretation of clastic depositional facies, in Seismic stratigraphy--Applications to hydrocarbon exploration, C. E. Payton, ed.: AAPG Mem. 26, Tulsa, Oklahoma, 516 p., 1977, p. 165-184.

Shepard, F. P., 1973, Submarine Geology, 3rd edn., 551 p., Harper and Row, New York.

Shipley, T. H., R. T. Buffler, and J. S. Watkins, 1978, Seismic stratigraphy and geologic history of Blake Plateau and adjacent western Atlantic continental margin: AAPG Bull., v. 62, p. 792-812.

Stuart, C. J., and C. A. Caughey, 1977, Seismic facies and sedimentology of terrigenous Pleistocene deposits in northwest and central Gulf of Mexico, in Seismic stratigraphy--Applications to hydrocarbon exploration, C. E. Payton, ed.: AAPG Mem. 26, Tulsa, Oklahoma, 516 p., 1977, p. 249-275.

Todd, R. G., and R. M. Mitchum, Jr., 1977, Seismic stratigraphy and global changes of sea level, part 8: Identification of Upper Triassic, Jurassic and Lower Cretaceous seismic sequences in Gulf of Mexico and offshore West Africa, in Seismic stratigraphy-- Applications to hydrocarbon exploration, C. E. Payton, ed.: AAPG Mem. 26, Tulsa, Oklahoma, 516 p., 1977, p. 145-163.

Uchupi, E., and K. O. Emery, 1967, Structure of continental margins of the United States: AAPG Bull., v. 51, p. 223-234.

_____, and K. O. Emery, 1968, Structure of continental margin off Atlantic coast of United States: AAPG Bull., v. 52, p. 1162-1193.

Vail, P. R., and R. M. Mitchum, Jr., 1977, Seismic stratigraphy and global changes in sea level, part 1: Overview, in Seismic stratigraphy--Applications to hydrocarbon exploration, C. E. Payton, ed.: AAPG Mem. 26, Tulsa, Oklahoma, 516 p., 1977, p. 51-52.

_____, R. M. Mitchum, Jr., and S. Thompson, III, 1977, Seismic stratigraphy and global changes of sea level, part 3: Relative changes of sea level from coastal onlap, in Seismic stratigraphy-- Applications to hydrocarbon exploration, C. E. Payton, ed.: AAPG Mem. 26, Tulsa, Oklahoma, 516 p., 1977, p. 63-81.

_____, R. M. Mitchum, Jr., and S. Thompson, III, 1977, Seismic-stratigraphy and global changes of sea level, part 4: Global cycles of relative changes of sea level, in Seismic stratigraphy-- Applications to hydrocarbon exploration, C. E. Payton, ed.: AAPG Mem. 26, Tulsa, Oklahoma, 516 p., 1977, p. 83-97.

Vail, P. R., R. M. Mitchum, Jr., R. G. Todd, J. M. Widmier, S. Thompson, III, J. B. Sangree, J. N. Bubb, and W. G. Hatlelid (listed in order of papers), 1977, Seismic stratigraphy and global changes of sea level, in Seismic stratigraphy--Applications to hydrocarbon exploration, C. E. Payton, ed.: AAPG Mem. 26, Tulsa, Oklahoma, 516 p., 1977.

_____, R. G. Todd, and J. B. Sangree, 1977, Seismic stratigraphy and global changes of sea level, part 5: Chronostratigraphic significance of seismic reflections, in Seismic stratigraphy--Applications to hydrocarbon exploration, C. E. Payton, ed.: AAPG Mem. 26, Tulsa, Oklahoma, 516 p., 1977, p. 99-116.

_____, et al., 1976, 1977, Various versions of short course notes, Stratigraphic interpretation of seismic data, AAPG school, Tulsa, Oklahoma.

Woodbury, H. O., I. B. Murray, Jr., P. J. Pickford, and W. H. Akers, 1973, Pliocene and Pleistocene depocenters, outer continental shelf, Louisiana and Texas: AAPG Bull., v. 57, p. 2428-2439.

Worzel, J. L., and C. A. Burk, 1978, Margins of Gulf of Mexico: AAPG Bull., v. 62, p. 2290-2307.

GEOLOGY
AND GEOMETRY
OF
DEPOSITIONAL SYSTEMS

L. F. Brown, Jr.
and W. L. Fisher

AUSTIN, TEXAS

1980

PREFACE

The role played by depositional systems and their component lithofacies in determining the geometry of impedance surfaces within a basin
is fundamental for seismic sequence and seismic facies analyses. The
seismic stratigrapher must be aware of the geometry and internal facies
composition of the principal depositional systems that fill sedimentary
basins. One or more contemporaneous depositional systems (fluvial,
delta, fan-delta, shelf or slope) comprise the principal stratigraphic
packages or elements of basin fill and, consequently, constitute seismic
(depositional) sequences. The sequences, which are bounded by erosional
or non-depositional unconformities, represent major depositional episodes
in the history of the basin. The nature and distribution of the successive
depositional system(s) constituting the principal seismic (depositional)
sequences in a basin provide the basis for interpreting the evolution of
tectonic and depositional style during the history of the basin. Recognition and delineation of these fundamental basin-fill units is called
seismic sequence analysis.

Within the seismic (depositional) sequence, lesser seismic reflection
units or seismic facies represent the seismic response to lithofacies
within a depositional system. Reflections in response to distinctive
stratal/lithic vertical sequences, configuration, and lateral continuity
can be further analyzed in terms of wave character (e.g., amplitude,
frequency), three-dimensional geometry, and bounding relationships to
permit the seismic stratigrapher to infer depositional process, environment,

and probable lithofacies composition. This further permits the interpreter to explain the velocity/density (impedance) geometry within the seismic facies in stratigraphic and depositional terms. Called seismic facies analysis, this procedure requires an understanding of the various litho- facies and their spatial distribution within respective depositional systems. It also requires an appreciation of gross depositional processes responsible for basin filling--progradation, aggradation, onlap, erosion, fill, drape, and slump, among others. Consequently, understanding genetic stratigraphy in all its ramifications is basic. The lithofacies (and equivalent seismic facies)become the fundamental stratigraphic unit. Of limited value is that part of traditional stratigraphy that emphasizes nomenclature and purely descriptive aspects of basin fill.

The spatial arrangement of depositional systems and component litho- facies is the basic data needed to infer reservoirs, seal, source and to develop stratigraphic and/or structural prospective trends.

This set of notes is composed of figures and captions summarizing the fundamental models and concepts needed to obtain a general perspective of sedimentary environments, processes and facies that characterize the various depositional systems. For many, this will be a review. For others, the concepts will be new. Nevertheless, this part of the course provides the stratigraphic basis for subsequent seismic stratigraphic interpretation.

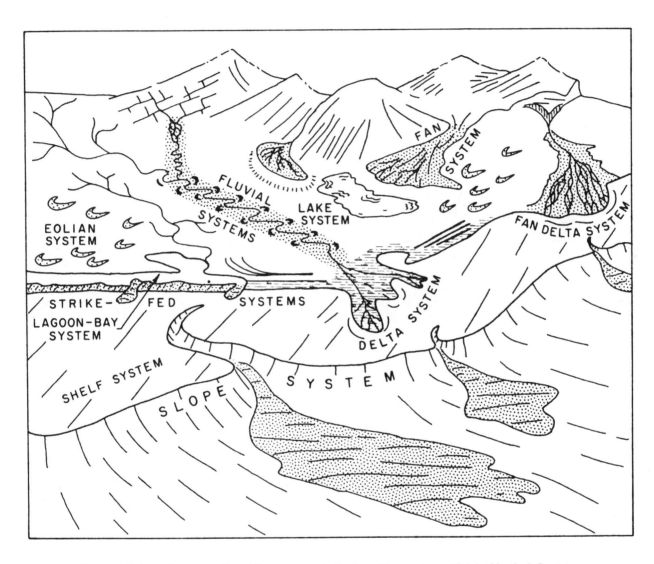

Figure 1. Schematic perspective of terrigenous clastic deposition systems. (Original by A. J. Scott.)

2

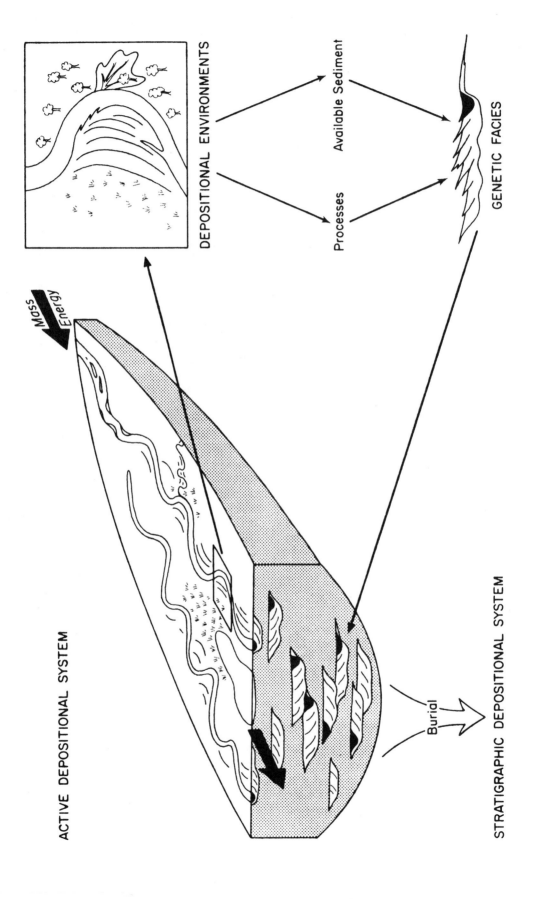

Figure 2. An active depositional system consists of genetically related environments. The sedimentary records of these environments, preserved as genetic facies, constitute a three-dimensional stratigraphic (ancient) depositional system. From Galloway and others (1978).

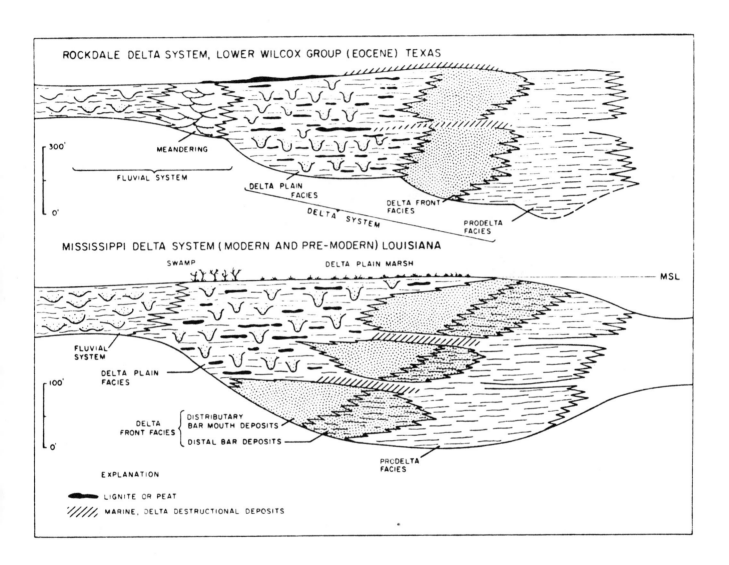

Figure 3. Comparison of component facies of Mississippi delta system (modified from partly hypothetical cross section in Coleman and Gagliano, 1964) and Rockdale Delta System, Lower Wilcox, Texas. Modified from Fisher and McGowen (1967). From Fisher (1969).

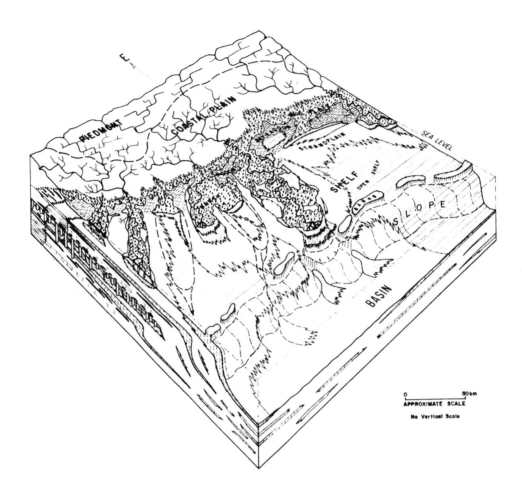

Figure 4. Distribution of principal depositional systems of the Eastern Shelf of the Midland Basin during Late Pennsylvanian time when deltaic, shelf, and slope systems were operative. After Brown (1969).

5

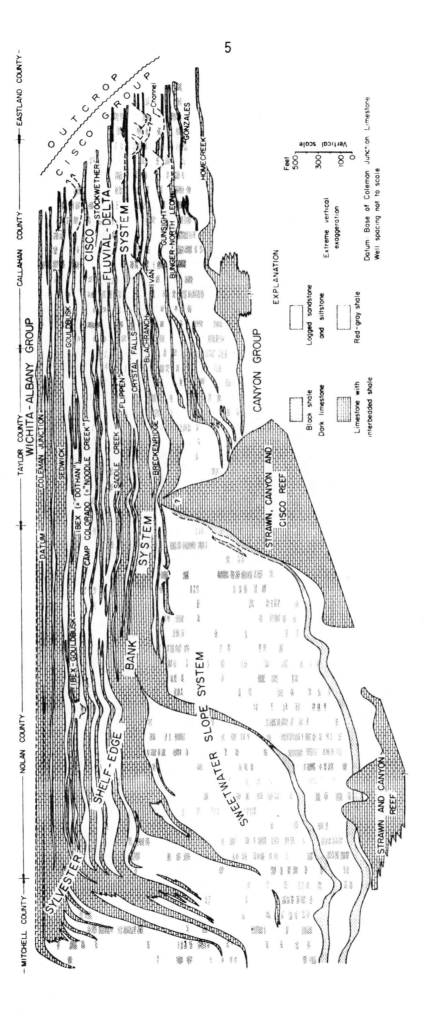

Figure 5. Cross section across the Eastern Shelf of the Midland Basin showing Cisco (Upper Pennsylvanian/Lower Permian) depositional systems. Based on 60 wells. After Brown (1969, 1973).

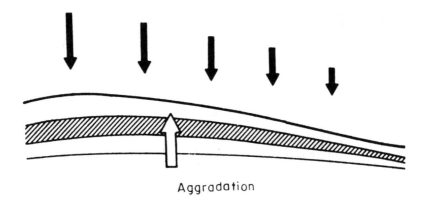

Aggradation

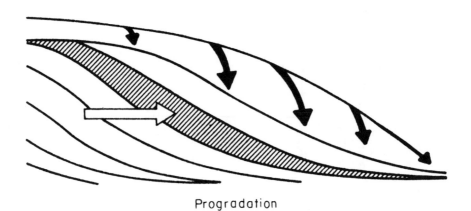

Progradation

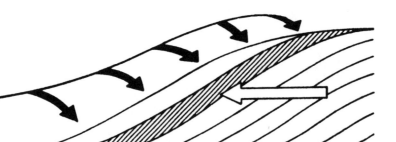

Lateral Accretion

Figure 6. Progradation, lateral accretion, and aggradation sedimentary processes, and geometries of resultant depositional units. After Galloway and others (1979).

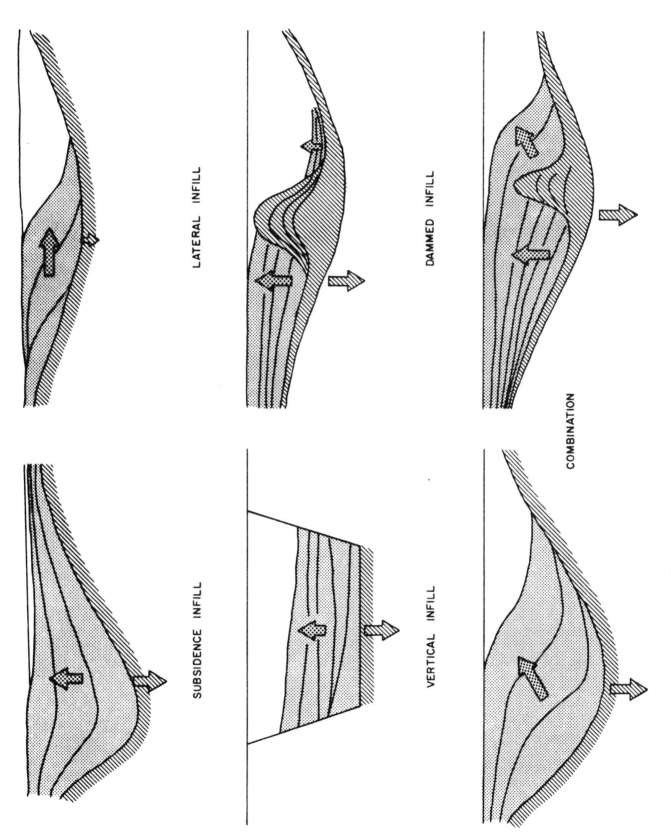

Figure 7. Architecture of typical basins showing the effect of the interplay of subsidence and depositional rates. After Galloway (unpublished).

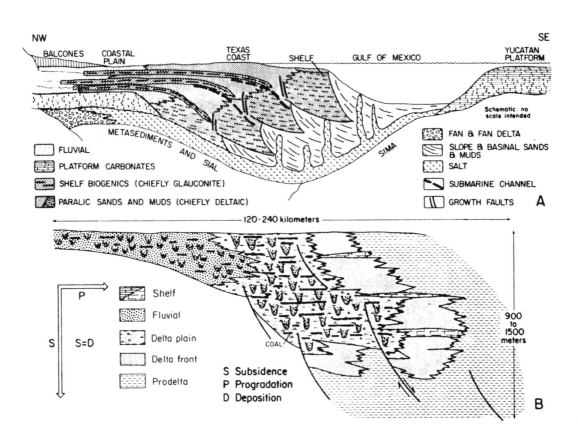

Figure 8. General characteristics of facies in northwestern part of the Gulf basin. (A) General cross section of Gulf basin showing principal depositional systems (modified from Lehner, 1969). (B) Dip cross section of Eocene delta system illustrating internal facies composition. After Fisher and McGowen (1967).

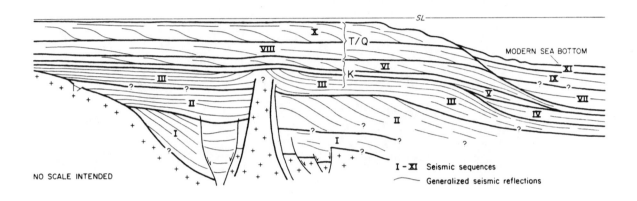

Figure 9. Generalized seismic sequences within the Baltimore Canyon area, U. S. Atlantic shelf. Based on U.S.G.S. Line 2 and COST B-2. Interpretation by A. M. de Figueiredo and M. V. Dauzacker (unpublished).

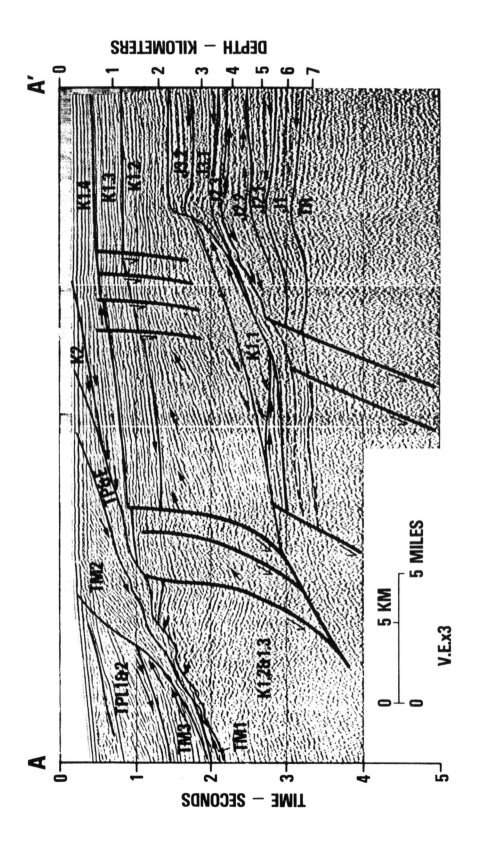

Figure 10. Seismic sequences from offshore northwest Africa showing sequences defined by seismic reflections. From Mitchum and others (1977).

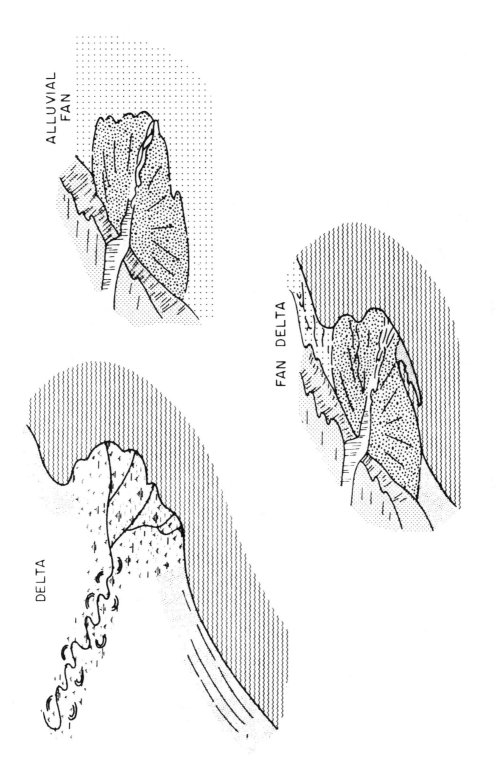

Figure 11. Schematic plan view of delta, alluvial fan, and fan delta systems.

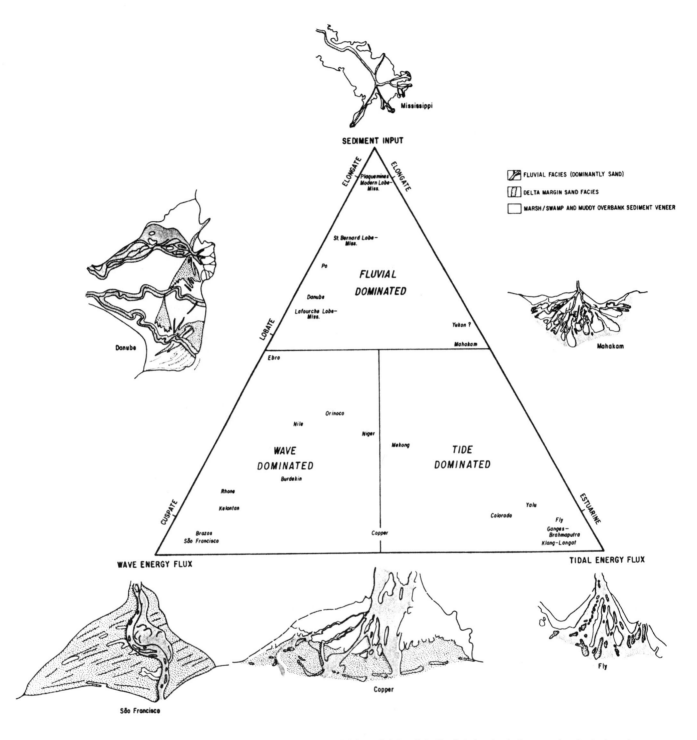

Figure 12. Schematic diagram illustrating the threefold division of deltas into fluvial-dominated, wave-dominated, and tide-dominated types. The relative importance of sediment input, wave energy flux, and tidal energy flux determine the morphology and internal stratigraphy of the delta. After Galloway (1975).

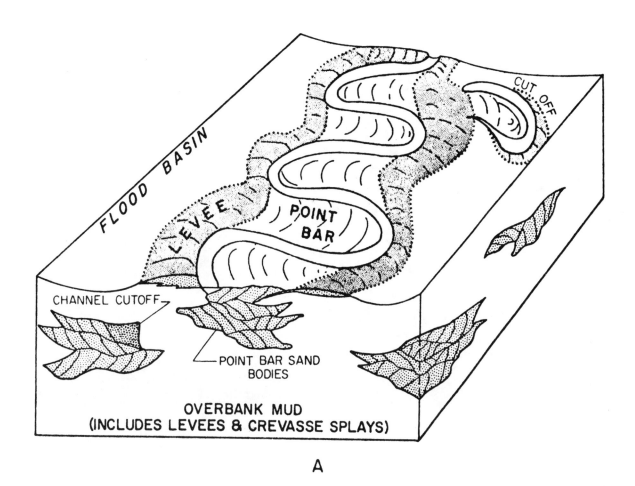

FLOOD BASIN

CUT OFF

LEVEE

POINT BAR

CHANNEL CUTOFF

POINT BAR SAND BODIES

OVERBANK MUD (INCLUDES LEVEES & CREVASSE SPLAYS)

A

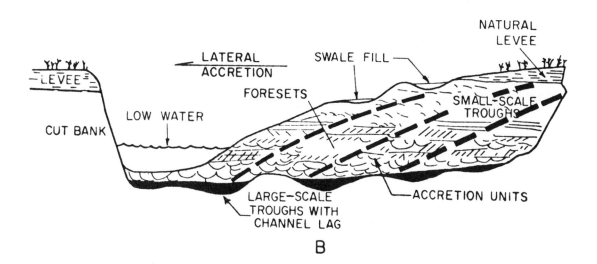

NATURAL LEVEE

LATERAL ACCRETION

SWALE FILL

FORESETS

SMALL-SCALE TROUGHS

LEVEE

LOW WATER

CUT BANK

LARGE-SCALE TROUGHS WITH CHANNEL LAG

ACCRETION UNITS

B

Figure 13. Depositional model of an idealized fine-grained meanderbelt fluvial system. (A) Block diagram showing bedforms, sedimentary structures, and multistory geometry; (B) Schematic cross section of fine-grained point-bar deposits. After Bernard and others (1963); described by Fisher and Brown (1972). From Brown (1973).

14

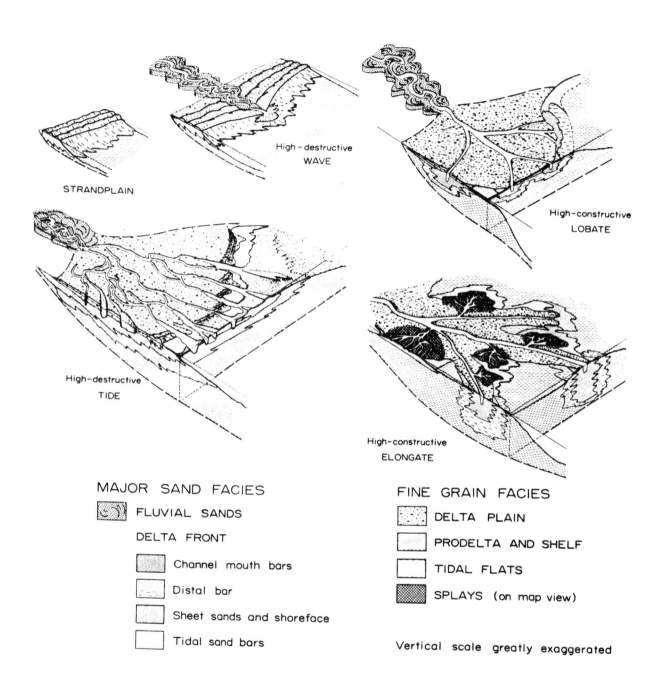

STRANDPLAIN

High-destructive
WAVE

High-constructive
LOBATE

High-destructive
TIDE

High-constructive
ELONGATE

MAJOR SAND FACIES

FLUVIAL SANDS

DELTA FRONT

Channel mouth bars

Distal bar

Sheet sands and shoreface

Tidal sand bars

FINE GRAIN FACIES

DELTA PLAIN

PRODELTA AND SHELF

TIDAL FLATS

SPLAYS (on map view)

Vertical scale greatly exaggerated

Figure 14. Framework facies in major types of deltas. (A) Strandplain, shown for comparison; (B) High-destructive wave composed primarily of shoreface and associated fluvial sands; (C) High-destructive tidal with extensive tidal shoal or sand flat facies; (D) High-constructive lobate with associated fluvial sands, channel mouth bars and delta front sheet sands; and (E) High-constructive elongate with thick channel mouth bars or bar fingers. After Fisher and others (1969).

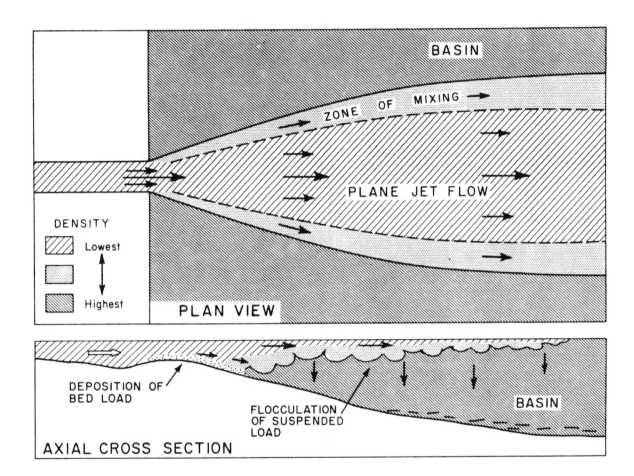

Figure 15. Hypopycnal flow. Plane jet flow with the reservoir fluid more dense than the inflowing fluid. This situation is characteristic of rivers flowing into oceans. Modified from Bates (1953). By A. J. Scott.

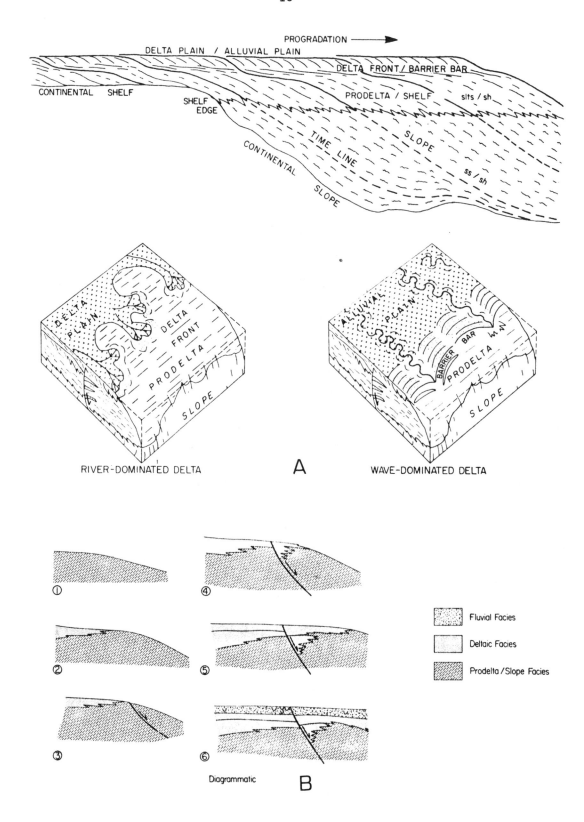

Figure 16. Delta depositional model illustrating the distribution of reservoir facies. (A) Generalized cross section of prograding delta system. Plan views of marine-dominated and river-dominated deltas demonstrate variations in lateral distribution of reservoir sand bodies. After Brown and Fisher (1977); (B) Stages of growth-fault development generated by shelf-margin delta system. After Galloway (1977).

17

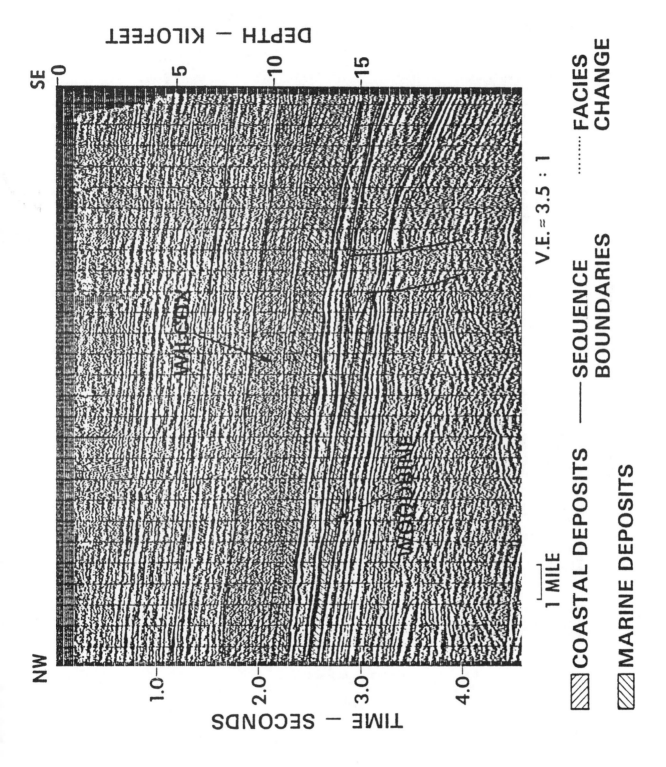

Figure 17. Seismic profile, East Texas. From Vail and others (1976). AAPG Seismic Stratigraphy course notes.

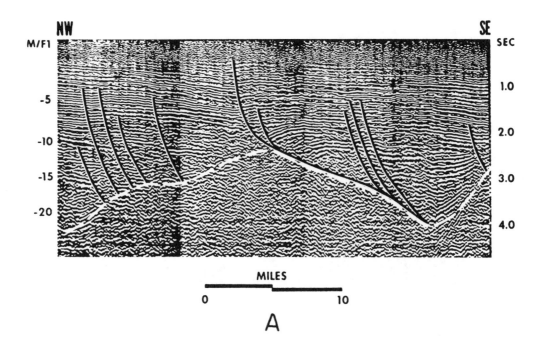

A

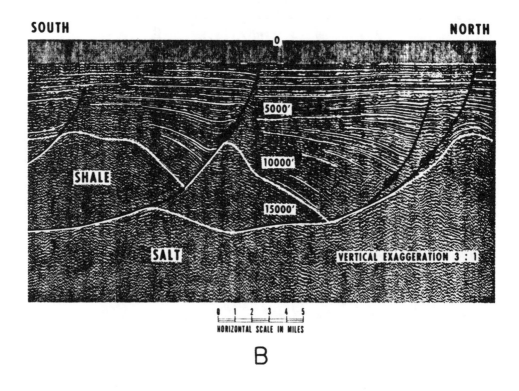

B

Figure 18. Seismic facies, growth faults, and shale diapirs characteristic of shelf-margin delta systems. (A) Tertiary delta systems of the Texas Gulf Coast basin. After Bruce (1973). (B) Plio-Pleistocene delta system Northern Gulf Coast basin. After Woodbury (1973).

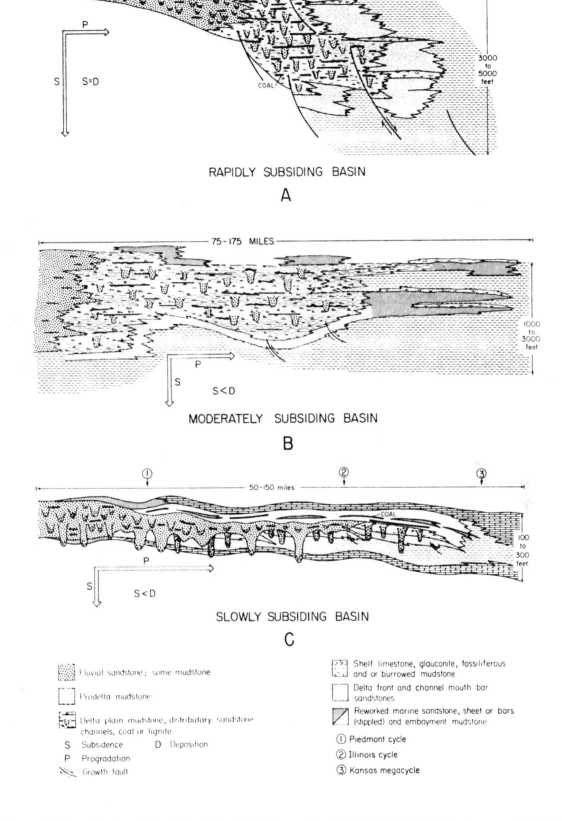

RAPIDLY SUBSIDING BASIN

A

MODERATELY SUBSIDING BASIN

B

SLOWLY SUBSIDING BASIN

C

Fluvial sandstone; some mudstone

Prodelta mudstone

Delta plain mudstone, distributary sandstone channels, coal or lignite

S Subsidence   D Deposition
P Progradation
Growth fault

Shelf limestone, glauconite, fossiliferous and or burrowed mudstone

Delta front and channel mouth bar sandstones

Reworked marine sandstone, sheet or bars (stippled) and embayment mudstone

① Piedmont cycle
② Illinois cycle
③ Kansas megacycle

Figure 19. Depositional models and the relationship between rates of subsidence/deposition and consequent degree of progradation. (A) Rapidly subsiding basin. After Fisher and McGowen (1967); (B) Moderately subsiding basin. After Weimer (1961); (C) Slowly subsiding basin. After Brown (1969).

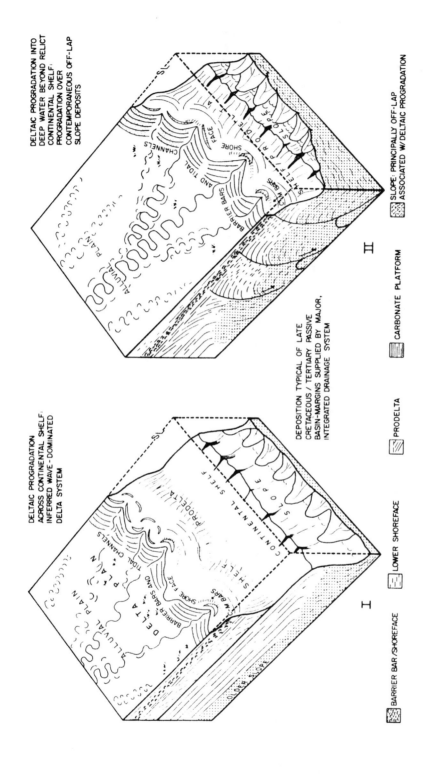

Figure 20. Generalized depositional model of delta/slope systems within Tertiary pull-apart, oceanic basins (Brazil and Africa) showing schematic representation of reflector attitudes and continuity. Deposition reflects development of an integrated drainage system resulting in the deposition of thick deltaic and slope facies. Prograding deltas built across subjacent carbonate platforms to shelf-edge positions where they supplied sediment that was redeposited by slope processes into deep-water environments. Note the growth faults and shale diapirs. After Brown and Fisher (1977).

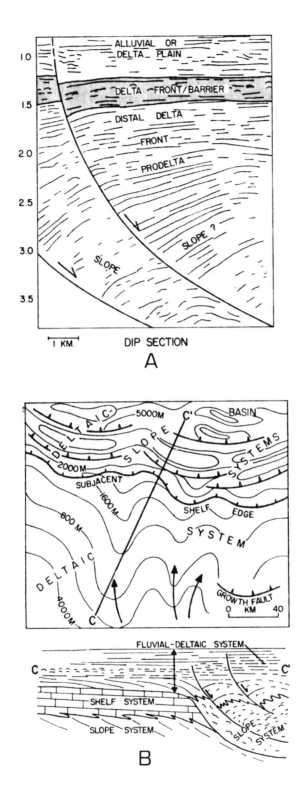

Figure 21. Generalized geometry of a delta system. (A) Contemporaneous growth fault typical of shelf-margin deltas. (B) Schematic cross section and isopach map of shelf and shelf-margin delta systems. After Brown and Fisher (1977).

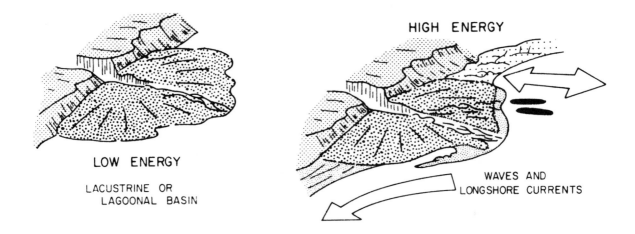

LOW ENERGY

LACUSTRINE OR
LAGOONAL BASIN

HIGH ENERGY

WAVES AND
LONGSHORE CURRENTS

Figure 22. Schematic sketch showing effect of marine energy on a fan-delta system.

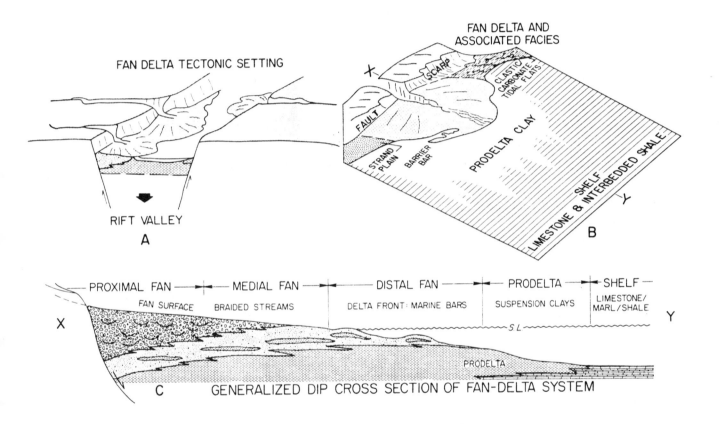

Figure 23. General setting, facies and facies associations that characterize fan-delta systems. (A) Common setting in rift basins; (B) Common association with carbonate facies and tidal flat/strandplain deposits; (C) Generalized cross section showing principal types of facies assemblages within the fan-delta system. After McGowen, unpublished. From Brown and Fisher (1976).

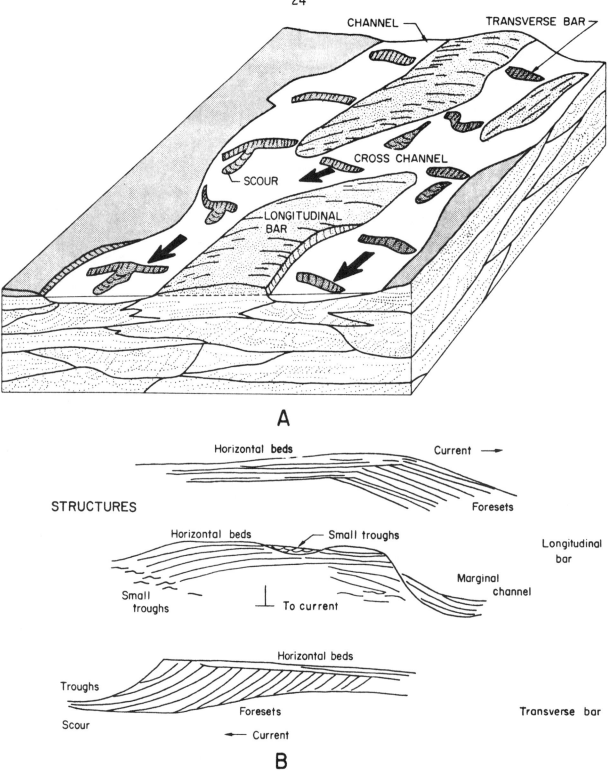

Figure 24. Depositional model of an idealized braided fluvial system. (A) Block diagram showing bedforms, sedimentary structures, and multilateral sand geometry; (B) Sedimentary structures deposited by longitudinal and transverse bars. Modified from Ore (1963, 1965) and Smith (1970); described by Fisher and Brown (1972). From Brown (1973).

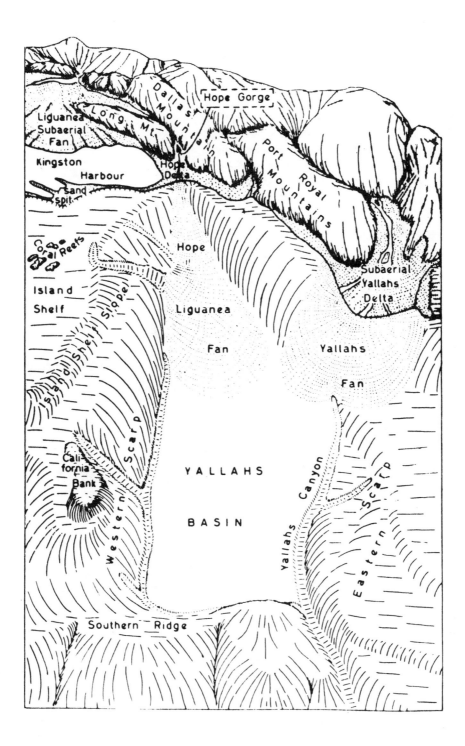

Figure 25. Depositional systems associated with the Yallahs Basin, south coast of Jamaica. After Burke (1967). Shows relationship of fan delta, carbonate, and turbidite systems.

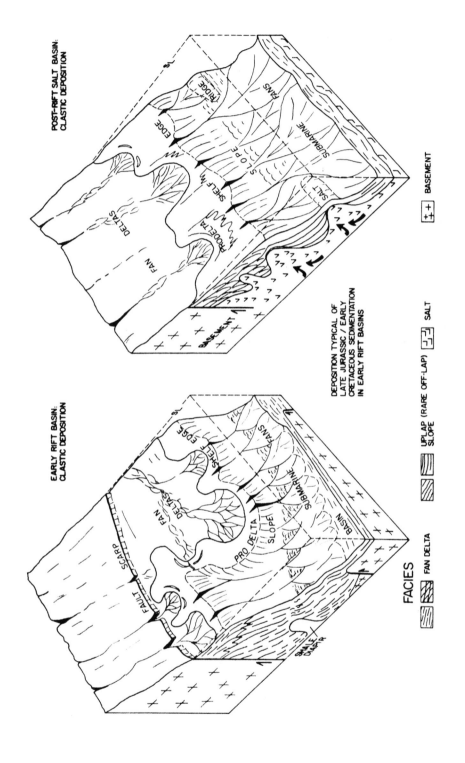

Figure 26. Generalized depositional models of a rift basin and salt-basin showing schematic representation of reflector attitudes and continuity. The rift-basin example is characterized by rapid deposition of fan-delta and slope facies within contemporaneously faulted basins; slope systems are commonly represented by offlap and uplap reflectors in response to rapid progradation and rapid subsidence. Similarly, fan-delta progradation across thick salt deposits produces salt mobilization resulting in salt dams and subsiding salt basins containing uplap facies. After Brown and Fisher (1977).

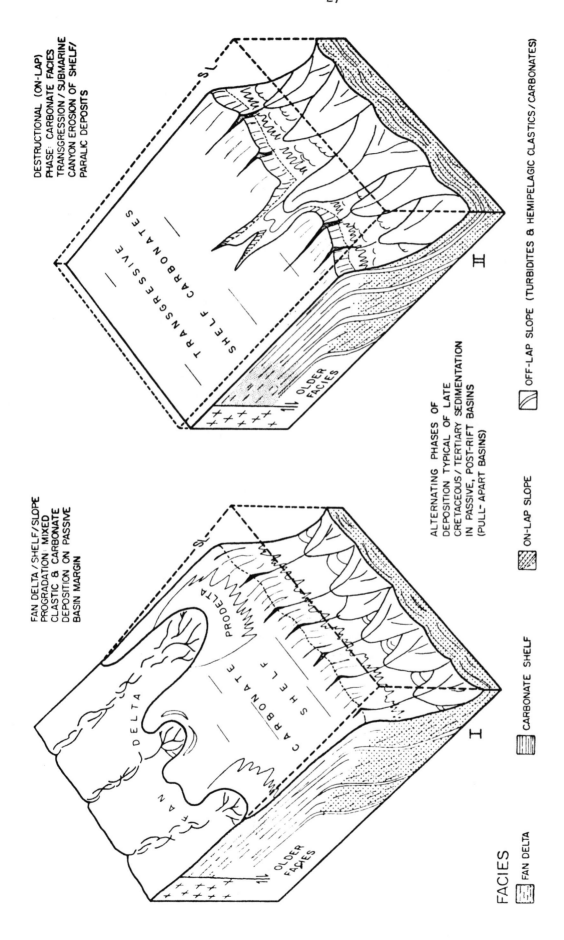

FAN DELTA / SHELF / SLOPE
PROGRADATION: MIXED
CLASTIC & CARBONATE
DEPOSITION ON PASSIVE
BASIN MARGIN

DESTRUCTIONAL (ON-LAP)
PHASE: CARBONATE FACIES
TRANSGRESSION / SUBMARINE
CANYON EROSION OF SHELF/
PARALIC DEPOSITS

ALTERNATING PHASES OF
DEPOSITION TYPICAL OF LATE
CRETACEOUS/ TERTIARY SEDIMENTATION
IN PASSIVE, POST-RIFT BASINS
(PULL-APART BASINS)

FACIES

FAN DELTA

CARBONATE SHELF

ON-LAP SLOPE

OFF-LAP SLOPE (TURBIDITES & HEMIPELAGIC CLASTICS / CARBONATES)

Figure 27. Generalized depositional model of fan-delta/carbonate shelf/slope systems within a passive, pull-apart basin showing schematic representation of reflector attitudes and continuity. Active fan-delta deposition supplied terrigenous clastic sediment to the shelf area where limestone deposition dominated; this sustained episode of clastic/carbonate sediment supply produced a steady progradation of offlap slope facies (I). Alternating with episodes of sustained progradation of shelf/slope environments were episodes of diminished sediment supply with corresponding erosion of shelf-edges and onlap of calcareous/clastic slope facies (II). After Brown and Fisher (1977).

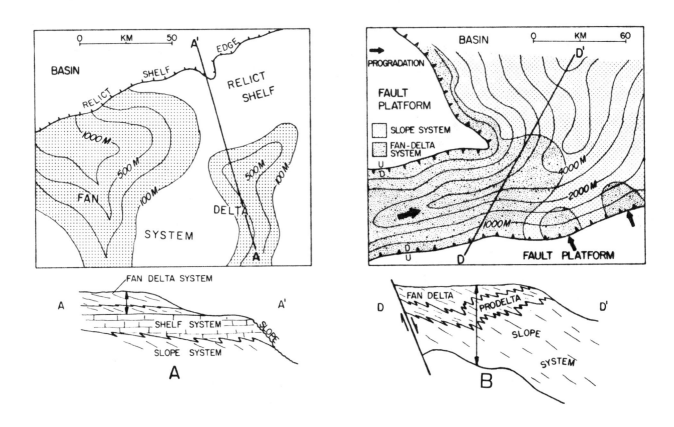

Figure 28. General geometry of fan delta systems. (A) Cross section and plan view of passive-margin fan delta system. (B) Cross section and plan view of rift-fill fan delta system. After Brown and Fisher (1977).

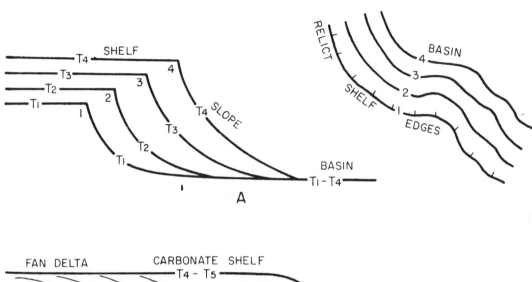

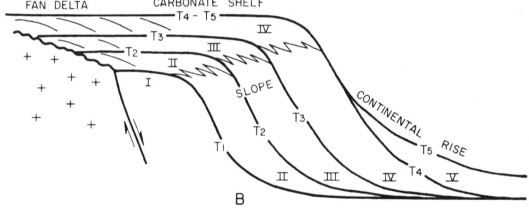

Figure 29. Diagrammatic representation of isochronous lines (surfaces) in hypothetical basins. (A) Progressive filling of a basin by shelf, slope and basinal deposition. (B) Fan-delta, carbonate shelf, and slope progradation with periodic continental rise (marine) onlap. After Brown and Fisher (1977).

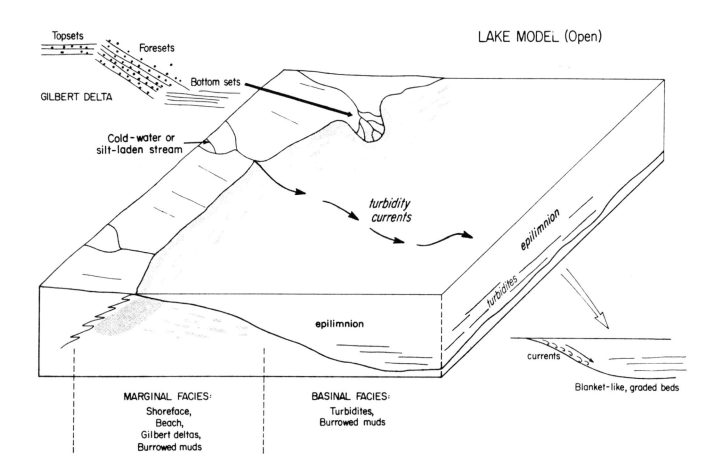

Figure 30. Open lake model. No permanent hypolimnion. Normal facies relationships.

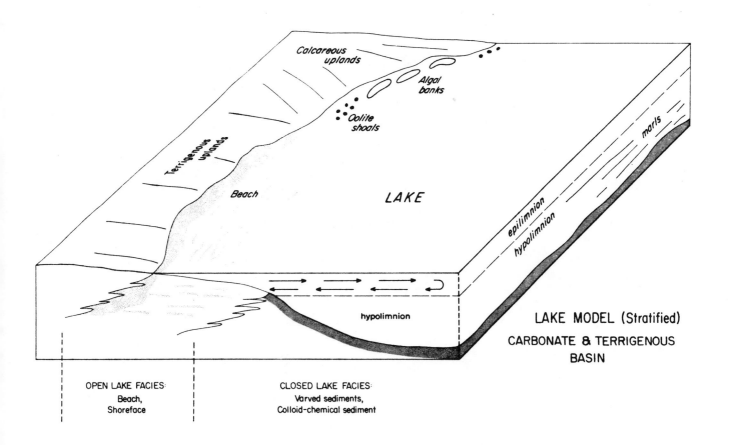

Figure 31. Closed or stratified lake model. Permanent or long-term hypolimnion. Exceedingly restricted conditions within the hypolimnion.

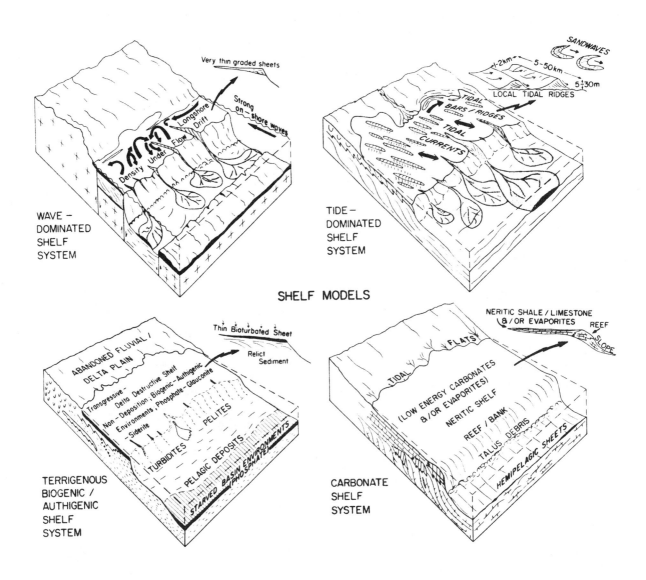

Figure 32. Conceptual shelf models illustrating biogenic/authigenic shelf, tide-dominated shelf, and carbonate shelf systems.

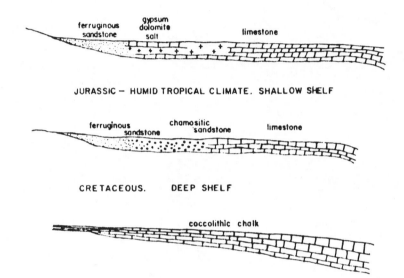

Figure 33. Mesozoic shelf systems of western Europe illustrating climatic and depth control. From Stanley (1969), modified from Hallum (1969).

34

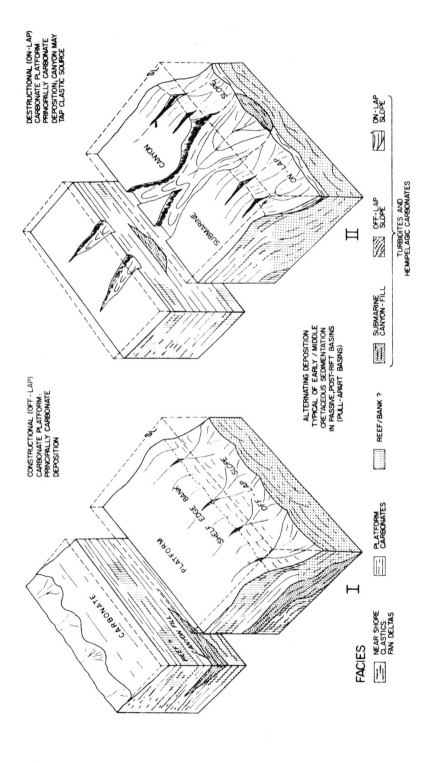

Figure 34. Generalized depositional model of carbonate platform complex within a post-rift, pull-apart basin showing schematic representation of reflector attitudes and continuity. See figures 9, 10, 15 for additional detail of reflector signatures. This early post-rift type of basin is characterized by offlapping shelf/slope systems of predominantly carbonate composition (I). Landward, minor fan-delta systems periodically supplied terrigenous sediment to the platform, but principal shelf/slope facies are limestone deposits. Shelf-edge reefs are common and the shelf-edge prograded by alternating deposition of calcareous offlap slope facies and onlap slope facies commonly associated with submarine canyon systems (II). After Brown and Fisher (1977).

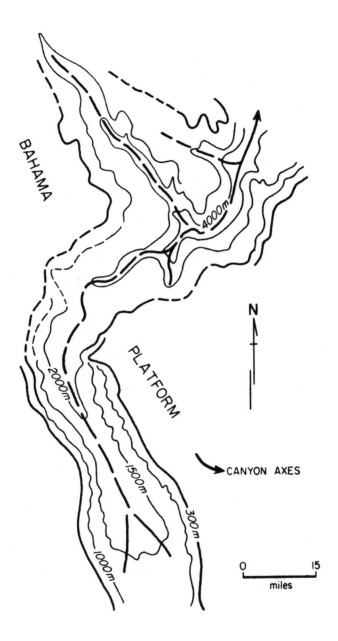

Figure 35. Tongue of the Ocean submarine canyon, Bahama platform. Shepard (1973).

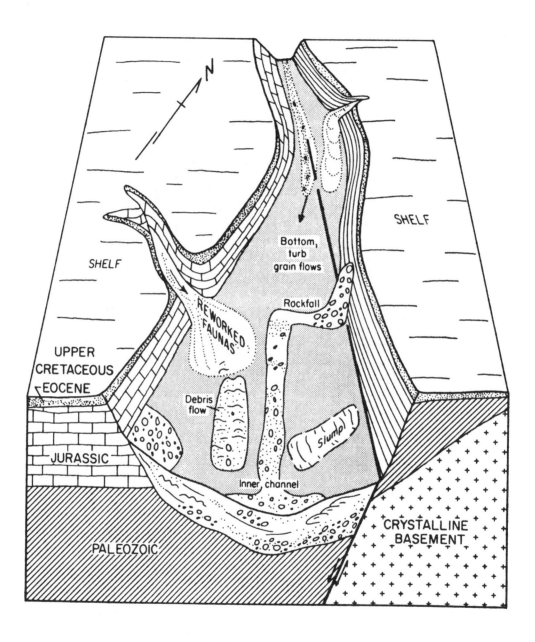

Figure 36. Major submarine canyon eroded more than 1,000 m into pre-Cenozoic strata and filled during Eocene and Oligocene. Czechoslovakia. From Picha (1979).

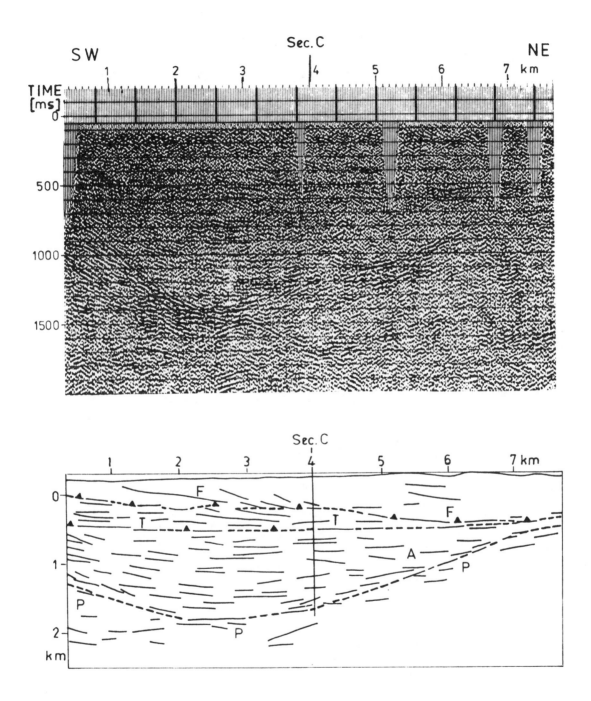

Figure 37. Time and depth sections of seismic reflection profile crossing Nesvacilka canyon, Czechoslovakia. A. autochthonous Paleogene canyon fill; T. tectonized Paleogene sediments related to canyon fill; F. Carpathian foldbelt; P. Paleozoic basement. After Picha (1979).

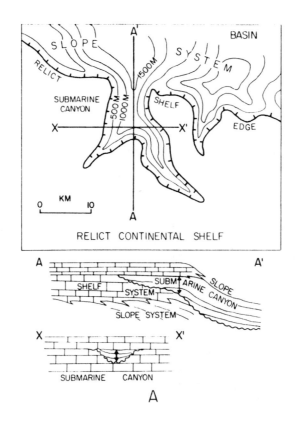

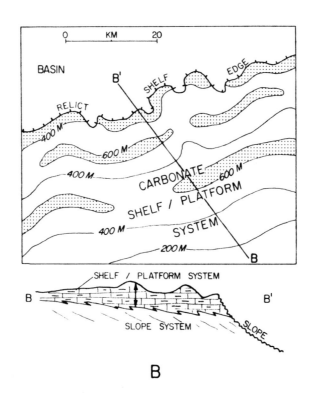

Figure 38. General geometry of carbonate platform systems. (A) Cross section and plan view of platform margin showing characteristic submarine canyon-fill deposits. (B) Cross section and plan view of carbonate platform illustrating strike-oriented relict shelf edge and bank elements of the system. After Brown and Fisher (1977).

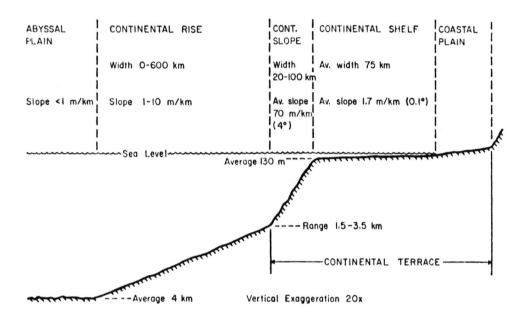

Figure 39. Diagrammatic profile of continental terrace, continental rise, and abyssal plain. From Curray (1965).

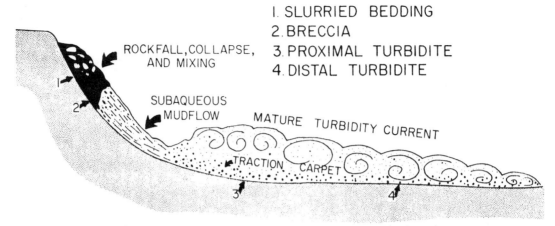

1. SLURRIED BEDDING
2. BRECCIA
3. PROXIMAL TURBIDITE
4. DISTAL TURBIDITE

A. POSSIBLE STRUCTURES FORMED BY FAILURE
OF PLASTIC MUDS AND FRIABLE SANDS

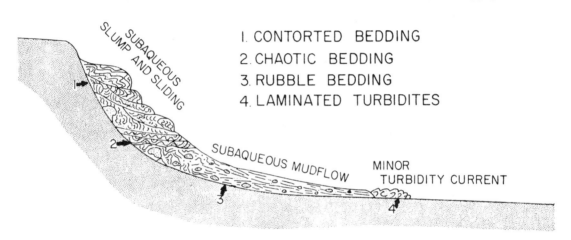

1. CONTORTED BEDDING
2. CHAOTIC BEDDING
3. RUBBLE BEDDING
4. LAMINATED TURBIDITES

B. POSSIBLE STRUCTURES FORMED BY FAILURE
OF PLASTIC MUDS AND COHESIVE SANDSTONES

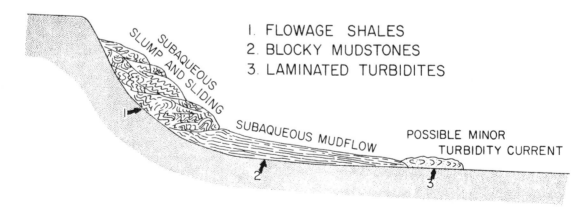

1. FLOWAGE SHALES
2. BLOCKY MUDSTONES
3. LAMINATED TURBIDITES

C. POSSIBLE STRUCTURES FORMED BY FAILURE
OF PLASTIC MUDS ONLY

Figure 40. Slope facies developed by submarine slump, slides, and rock falls. Based on Mississippian Jackfork flysch facies, Oklahoma. From Morris (1971).

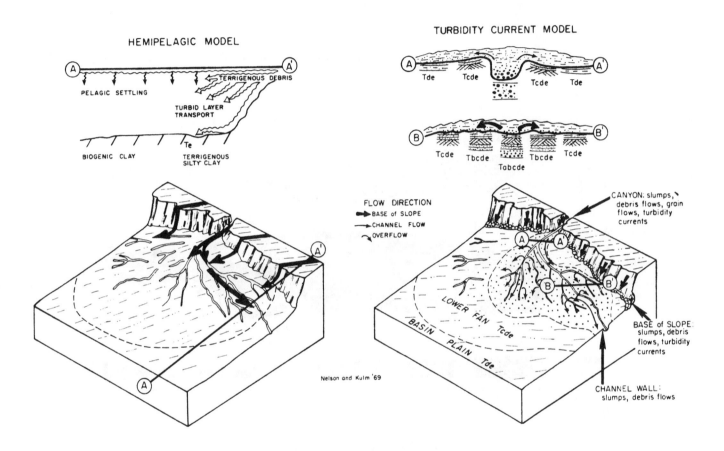

Figure 41. Models of hemipelagic and turbidity current processes on submarine fans. From Nelson and Kulm (1973).

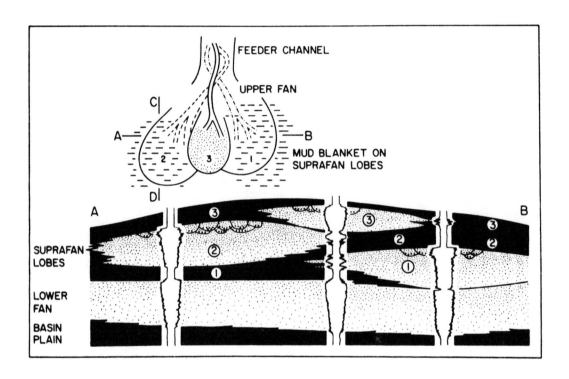

Figure 42. Hypothetical cross section across progradational mid and lower submarine fan facies. Simulated electric logs. From Walker (1978).

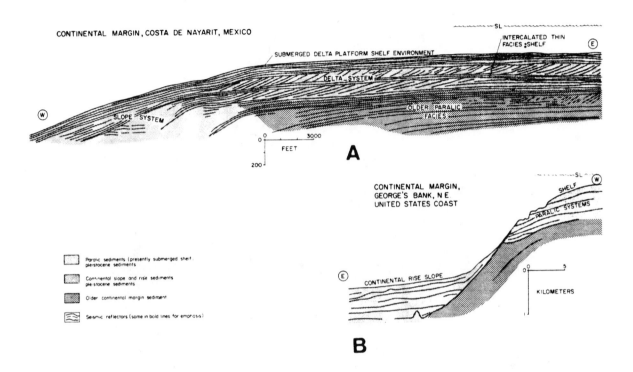

Figure 43. Seismic profiles of Pleistocene offlap and onlap slope systems. (A) Offlap slope, western Mexico continental margin. From Curray and Moore (1964). (B) Onlap (continental rise) slope, U. S. Atlantic margin. From Uchupi and Emery (1967).

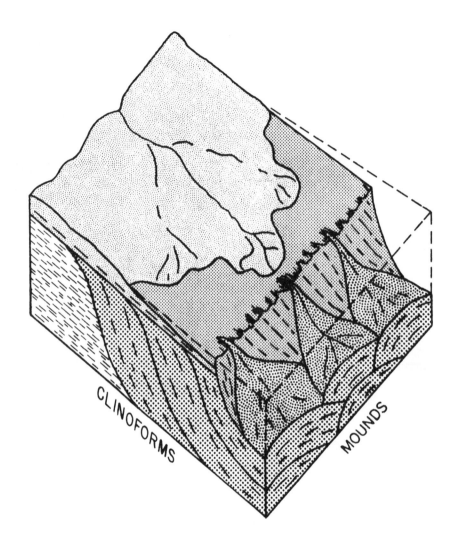

Figure 44. Relationship of progradational (dip) and mounded (strike) stratal/reflector configuration. Indicates diachronous nature of individual, shifting slope mounds or cones.

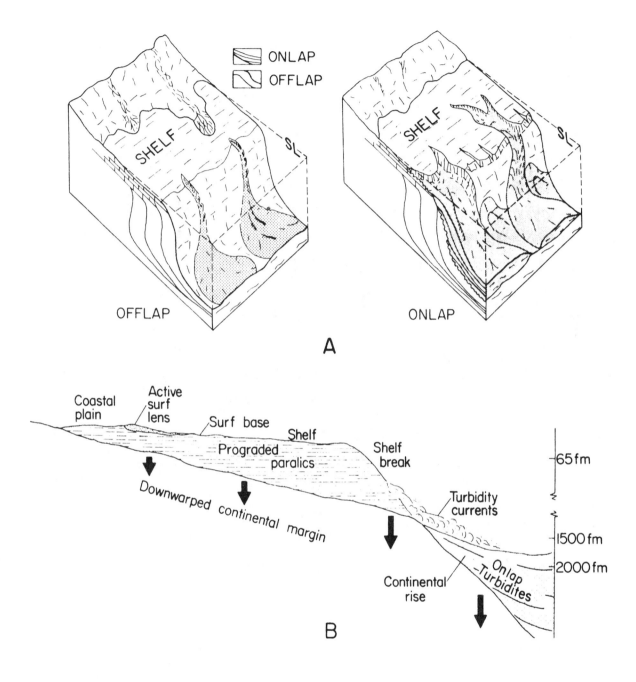

Figure 45. The nature of offlap and onlap deposition, two fundamental depositional styles that characterize many slope systems. (A) Block diagrams that illustrate general processes: offlap occurs during sustained sediment supply provided by deltas, fan-deltas, and highly productive shelf-edge carbonate environments; onlap conversely occurs when sediment supply diminishes and erosional processes rework shelf or paralic sediments, commonly via submarine canyons. Offlap reflectors reflect the basinward progradation of slope deposits, and onlap reflectors mark periods of landward recession of slope depocenters. (B) Schematic representation of onlap processes. After Dietz (1963).

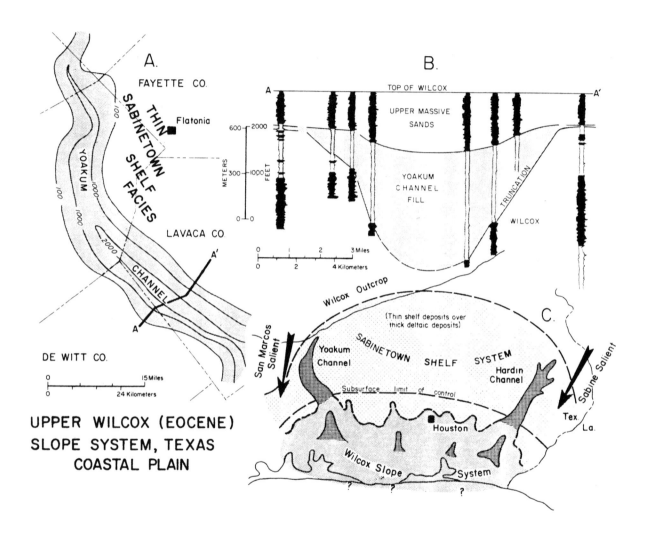

Figure 46. Upper Wilcox (Eocene) slope system and associated Yoakum and Hardin canyons, Texas Gulf Coast basin. Modified from Hoyt (1959) by W. L. Fisher.

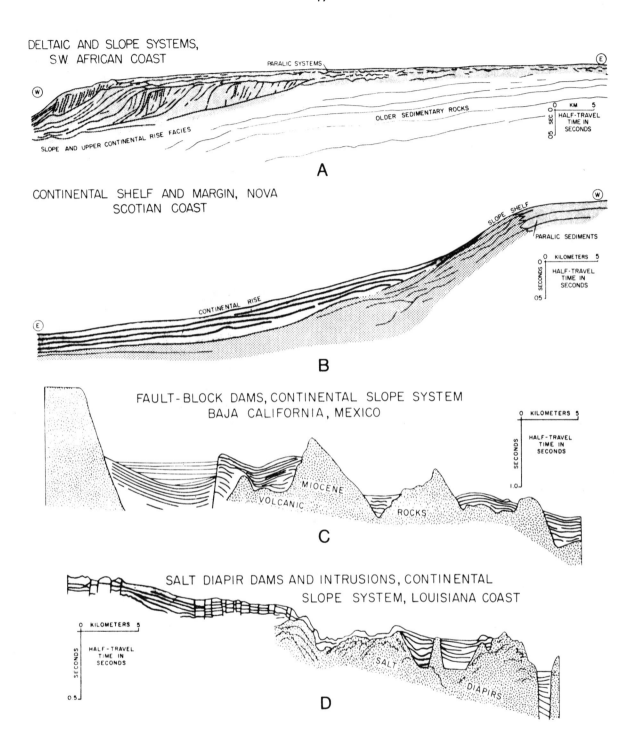

DELTAIC AND SLOPE SYSTEMS,
S.W. AFRICAN COAST

PARALIC SYSTEMS

Ⓔ

Ⓦ

OLDER SEDIMENTARY ROCKS

KM 5

HALF-TRAVEL
TIME IN
SECONDS

SLOPE AND UPPER CONTINENTAL RISE FACIES

A

CONTINENTAL SHELF AND MARGIN, NOVA
SCOTIAN COAST

Ⓦ

SLOPE SHELF

PARALIC SEDIMENTS

KILOMETERS 5

HALF-TRAVEL
TIME IN
SECONDS

CONTINENTAL RISE

Ⓔ

B

FAULT-BLOCK DAMS, CONTINENTAL SLOPE SYSTEM
BAJA CALIFORNIA, MEXICO

KILOMETERS 5

HALF-TRAVEL
TIME IN
SECONDS

MIOCENE
VOLCANIC
ROCKS

C

SALT DIAPIR DAMS AND INTRUSIONS, CONTINENTAL
SLOPE SYSTEM, LOUISIANA COAST

KILOMETERS 5

HALF-TRAVEL
TIME IN
SECONDS

SALT

DIAPIRS

D

Figure 47. General nature of seismic reflectors that characterize several styles of deposition along some Holocene continental margins. (A) Complex reflector patterns within deltaic and slope systems along the southwestern African coast. After McMaster and others (1970). (B) Continental rise onlap along the Nova Scotian coast. After Uchupi and Emery (1967). (C) Fault basins containing superposed (uplap) slope deposits dammed behind fault blocks, Baja California, Mexico. After Emery (1970). (D) Slope deposits trapped within salt basins and behind salt ridges along the Louisiana coast, Gulf of Mexico. After Uchupi and Emery (1968).

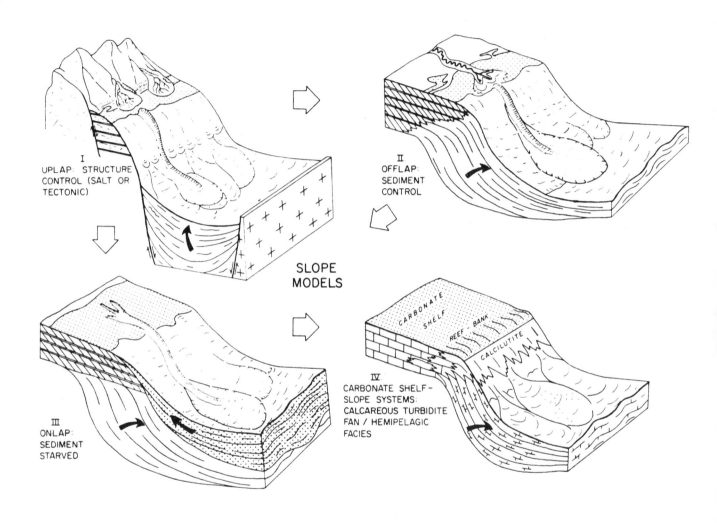

Figure 48. Examples of slope deposition within basins influenced by different tectonic styles and sediment supply. During the development of a basin, each depositional type may occur. The onlap type may develop when sediment supply diminishes periodically. Within rift and post-rift basins, there is commonly a progression from Type I to Type II and eventually to Type IV, with periodic episodes during which Type III may develop. Modified from Brown and Fisher (1977).

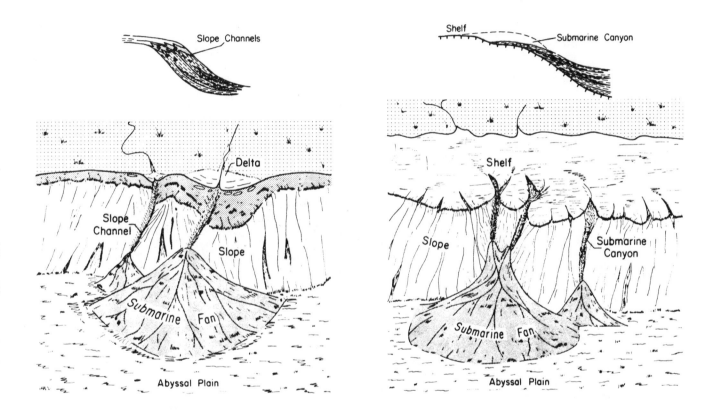

Figure 49. Schematic representation of slope deposition supplied by shelf-margin delta (left) and by erosion of shelf/slope. Modified from Moore and Asquith (1971).

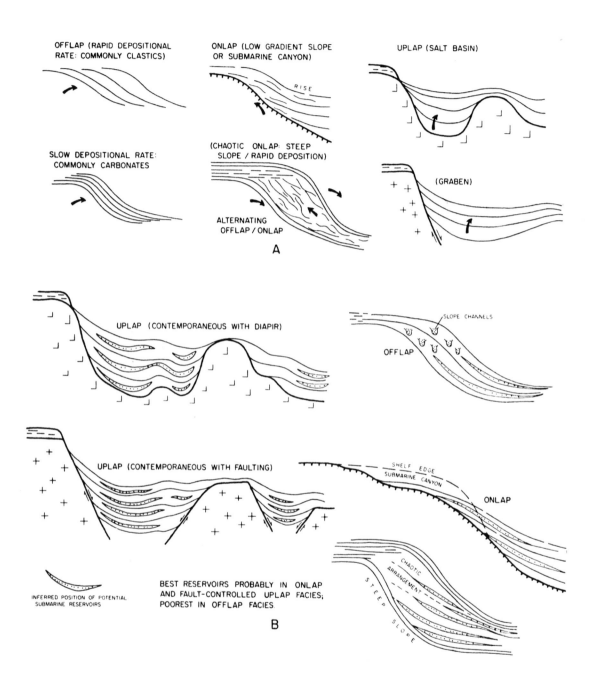

Figure 50. Seismic-stratigraphic slope facies patterns and the inferred distribution of submarine fan reservoirs. (A) Schematic representation of reflector patterns that characterize offlap, onlap, and uplap slope facies. (B) Inferred distribution of submarine fan sandstone facies within the three principal types of slope systems. After Brown and Fisher (1977).

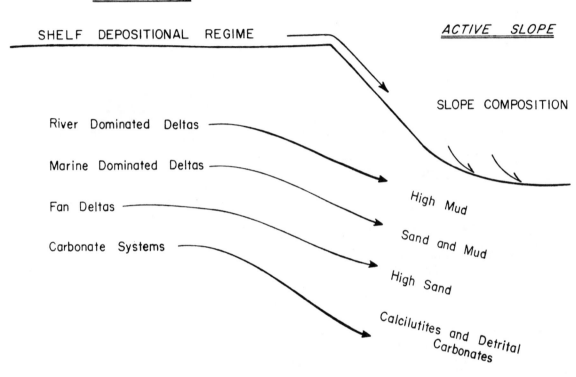

FACTORS IN SLOPE COMPOSITION
DIRECT FEEDING: OFFLAP

ACTIVE SHELF

SHELF DEPOSITIONAL REGIME

ACTIVE SLOPE

SLOPE COMPOSITION

River Dominated Deltas

Marine Dominated Deltas

Fan Deltas

Carbonate Systems

High Mud

Sand and Mud

High Sand

Calcilutites and Detrital Carbonates

Figure 51. Probable composition of offlap on progradational slope facies supplied by various active shallow marine systems.

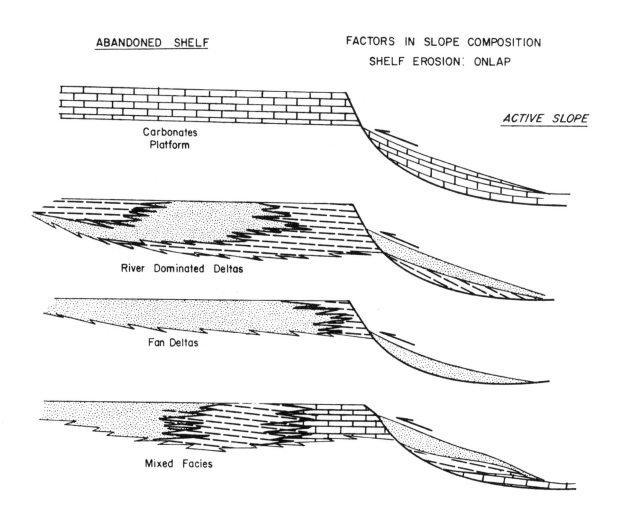

Figure 52. Probable composition of onlap slope facies associated with various relict shallow marine facies. This model implies a destructive, sediment-starved origin for onlap slope systems.

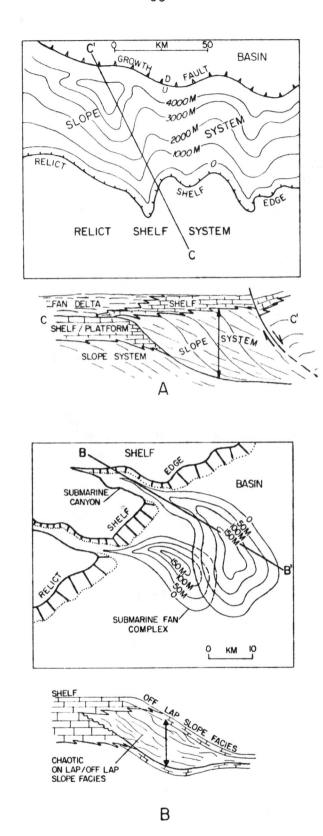

Figure 53. General geometry of slope systems. (A) Cross section and plan view of slope system. (B) Cross section and plan view of individual submarine fan geometry. After Brown and Fisher (1977).

REFERENCES

Bates, C. C., 1953, Rational theory of delta formation: AAPG Bull.,
    v. 37 pp. 2119-2162.

Bernard, H. A. and C. F. Major, Jr., 1963, Recent meanderbelt deposits
    of the Brazos River: and alluvial "sand" model : AAPG Bull.,
    v. 47, p. 350.

Brown, L. F., Jr., 1969, Geometry and distribution of fluvial and deltaic
    sandstones (Pennsylvanian and Permian), North-Central Texas: Trans.
    Gulf Coast Assoc. Geol. Socs., v. 19, pp. 23-47.

Brown, L. F., Jr., A. W. Cleaves, II, and A. W. Erxleben, 1973,
    Pennsylvanian depositional systems in North-Central Texas: Univ.
    Texas Bur. Econ. Geology Guidebook 14, 122 p.

Brown, L. F., Jr., and W. L. Fisher, 1976, Seismic facies reflection
    patterns: examples from Brazilian rift and pull-apart basins, in
    Stratigraphic interpretation of seismic data: AAPG and SEG, short
    course notes, Tulsa, pp. 48.

Brown, L. F., Jr., and W. L. Fisher, 1977, Seismic stratigraphic inter-
    pretation of depositional systems: Examples from Brazilian rift
    and pull-apart basins, in Seismic stratigraphy-Applications to
    hydrocarbon exploration, C. E. Payton, ed.: AAPG MEM. 26, pp. 213-
    248.

Bruce, C. H., 1973, Pressured shale and related sediment deformation:
    mechanism for development of regional contemporaneous faults: AAPG
    Bull., v. 57, pp. 878-886.

Burke, Kevin, 1967, The Yallahs Basin: a sedimentary basin southeast of
    Kingston, Jamaica: Marine Geology, v. 5, pp. 5-60.

Curray, J. R. and D. G. Moore, 1964, Pleistocene deltaic progradation of
    continental terrace, Costa de Nayarit, Mexico, in Marine geology
    of the Gulf of California: a symposium: AAPG Mem. 3, p. 193-215.

Curray, J. R., 1965, Late Quaternary history, continental shelves of the
    United States, Princeton Univ. Press, p. 723-735.

Dietz, 1963, Collapsing continental rises: an actualistic concept of
    geosynclines and mountain building: Jour. Geol., v. 71, p. 314-333.

Emery, K. O., 1970, Continental margins of the world, in The geology of
    the east Atlantic continental margins: part 1. General and economic
    papers, F. M. Delany, ed., Rept. No. 70-13, Natural Environment
    Research Council, Institute of Geological Science, p. 3-29.

Fisher, W. L., 1969, Facies characterization of Gulf Coast Basin delta
    systems, with Holocene analogues: Trans. Gulf Coast Assoc. Geol.
    Socs., v. 19, pp. 239-261.

Fisher, W. L. and J. H. McGowen, 1967, Depositional systems in the Wilcox Group of Texas and their relationship to occurrence of oil and gas: Trans. Gulf Coast Assoc. Geol. Socs., v. 17, pp. 105-125.

Fisher, W. L., L. F. Brown Jr., A. J. Scott, and J. H. McGowen, 1969, Delta systems in the exploration for oil and gas: a research colloquium: Univ. Texas Bur. Econ. Geology, 102 p. text, 168 figs.

Fisher, W. L. and L. F. Brown, Jr., 1972, Clastic depositional systems- a genetic approach to facies analysis (Annotated outline and bibliography): Univ. Texas Bur. Econ. Geology, 211 p.

Galloway, W. E., 1975, Process framework for describing the morphologic and stratigraphic evolution of deltaic depositional systems in Deltas, models for exploration, (M. L. Broussard, ed.): Houston Geological Society, Houston, pp. 87-98.

Galloway, W. E., 1977, Catahoula Formation of the Texas Coastal Plain: depositional systems, composition, structural development, ground-water flow history, and uranium distribution: Univ. Texas Bur. Econ. Geol., Rep. of Inv. No. 87, 59 p.

Galloway, W. E., R. J. Finley, and C. D. Henry, 1979, South Texas uranium province--geologic perspective: Univ. Texas Bur. Econ. Geology, Guidebook 18, 81 p.

Galloway, W. E., Charles W. Kreitler, and J. H. McGowen, 1978, Depositional and ground-water flow systems in the exploration for uranium: a research colloquium: Univ. Texas Bur. Econ. Geology, 267 p., reprinted 1979.

Hallum, A., 1969, Aspects of Mesozoic shelf in Western Europe: Program, 1969 Annual Meeting, AAPG, p. 67.

Hoyt, W. V., 1959, Erosional channel in the middle Wilcox near Yoakum, Lavaca County, Texas: Trans. Gulf Coast Assoc. Geol., v. 9, p. 41-50.

Lehner, P., 1969 Salt tectonics and Pleistocene stratigraphy on continental slope of northern Gulf of Mexico: AAPG Bull., v. 53, p. 2431-2497.

McMasters, R. L., and T. P. LaChance, 1969, Northwestern African continental shelf sediments: Marine Geology, v. 7, p. 57-67.

Mitchum, R. M. and P. R. Vail, 1977, Seismic stratigraphy and global changes of sea level, part 7: Seismic stratigraphic interpretation procedure, in Seismic stratigraphy - Applications to hydrocarbon exploration, C. E. Payton, ed.: AAPG Memoir 26, Tulsa Oklahoma, 516 p. 1977.

Moore, G. T. and D. O. Asquith, 1971, Delta: term and concept: Geol. Soc. Am. Bull., v. 82, p. 2563-2568.

Morris, R. C., 1971, Stratigraphy and sedimentology of Jack Fork Group, Arkansas: AAPG Bull., v. 55, p. 387-402.

Nelson, C. H. and L. D. Kulm, 1973, Submarine fans and deep-sea channels, in Turbidites and deep water sedimentation, G. V. Middleton and A. H. Bonna, co-chairmen: Pacific Section, Soc. Econ. Paleon. Min., Los Angeles, p. 39-78.

Ore, H. T., 1963, Some criteria for recognition of braided stream deposits: Univ. Wyoming, Contr. to Geology, v. 3, pp. 1-14.

Ore, H. T., 1965, Characteristic deposits of rapidly aggrading streams: Wyoming Geol. Assoc., 19th Field Conf. Guidebook, pp. 195-201.

Picha, F., 1979, Ancient submarine canyons of Tethyan continental margins, Czechoslovakia: AAPG Bull., v. 63, p. 67-86.

Shepard, F. P., 1973, Submarine Geology, 3rd ed., Harper and Row, New York, 551 p.

Smith, N. D., 1970, The braided stream depositional environment: comparison of the Platte River with some Silurian clastic rocks, north-central Appalachians: Bull. Geol. Soc. America, v. 81, pp. 2993-3014.

Stanley, D. J. (ed.), 1969, The new concepts of continental margin sedimentation: Application to the Geologic Record: short course lecture notes, American Geologic Institute, Washington D. C.

Uchupi, E. and K. O. Emery, 1967, Structure of continental margins of the United States: AAPG Bull., v. 51, p. 223-234.

Uchupi, E., and K. O. Emery, 1968, Structure of the continental margin off Atlantic coast of United States: AAPG Bull., v. 52, p. 1162-1193.

Vail, P. R., R. M. Mitchum, Jr., R. G. Todd, J. M. Widmier, S. Thompson, III J. B. Sangree, J. N. Bubb, and W. G. Hatlelid, 1977, Seismic stratigraphy and global changes of sea level, in Seismic stratigraphy - Applications to hydrocarbon exploration, C. E. Payton, ed.: AAPG Mem. 26, Tulsa, Okla., 516 p.

Walker, R. G., 1978, Deep-water sandstone facies and ancient submarine fans: Models for exploration for stratigraphic traps: AAPG Bull., v. 62, p. 932-966.

Weimer, R. J., 1961, Upper most Cretaceous rocks in central and southern Wyoming and northwestern Colorado, in Symposium on Late Cretaceous rocks, Wyoming and adjacent areas, Wyoming Geol. Assoc., 16th Ann. Field Conf., Casper, Wyoming, Petroleum. Inf., pp. 17-28.

Woodbury, H. O., I. B. Murray, Jr., P. J. Pickford, and W. H. Akers, 1973, Pliocene and Pleistocene depocenters, outer continental shelf, Louisiana and Texas: AAPG Bull., v. 57, p. 2428-2439.